CW01496589

Corpus and Context

Studies in Corpus Linguistics (SCL)

SCL focuses on the use of corpora throughout language study, the development of a quantitative approach to linguistics, the design and use of new tools for processing language texts, and the theoretical implications of a data-rich discipline.

Volume 30

Corpus and Context. Investigating pragmatic functions in spoken discourse
by Svenja Adolphs

Corpus and Context

Investigating pragmatic functions
in spoken discourse

Svenja Adolphs
University of Nottingham

John Benjamins Publishing Company

Amsterdam / Philadelphia

™ The paper used in this publication meets the minimum requirements of
American National Standard for Information Sciences – Permanence of
Paper for Printed Library Materials, ANSI z39.48-1984.

Library of Congress Cataloging-in-Publication Data

Adolphs, Svenja.
  Corpus and context : investigating pragmatic functions in spoken discourse / Svenja
    Adolphs.
    p. cm. (Studies in Corpus Linguistics, ISSN 1388-0373 ; v. 30)
Includes bibliographical references and index.
1. Discourse analysis--Data processing. 2. Corpora (Linguistics) 3. Speech acts
    (Linguistics) 4. Pragmatics. I. Title.
P302.3.A355   2008
401'.410285--dc22   2007045722
ISBN 978 90 272 2304 3 (Hb; alk. paper)

John Benjamins Publishing Co. · P.O. Box 36224 · 1020 ME Amsterdam · The Netherlands
John Benjamins North America · P.O. Box 27519 · Philadelphia PA 19118-0519 · USA

Table of contents

Acknowledgements

The use of spoken corpora to study pragmatic patterns of speech act expressions was an idea that John Sinclair shared with me during a workshop at the Tuscan Word Centre in the 1990s. It later became the topic of my PhD thesis which forms the basis of this publication. Ronald Carter supervised my thesis and I am greatly indebted to him for his unstinting help, guidance and encouragement. He has been extremely generous with his time and ideas in providing feedback on this work and subsequent research. I have also benefited greatly from the detailed comments provided by the thesis examiners, Mike McCarthy and Guy Cook, and I am grateful to them for raising interesting issues and points of discussion in relation to this work.

I have been very fortunate to be able to draw on the expertise of colleagues here at the University of Nottingham and the IVACS research group while writing this book. I am grateful to them for providing helpful feedback on different ideas and projects that are discussed in this volume.

Special thanks to Dawn Knight who has been instrumental in the research on language and gesture covered in Chapter 6, and to Phoebe Lin who has been a great help in preparing the final version of the manuscript for publication.

Thanks also to Elena Tognini-Bonelli, Kees Vaes and Martine van Marsbergen who provided huge and invaluable support for this project and who have been a real pleasure to work with.

The research discussed in Chapter 6 is funded by the UK Economic and Social Research Council (ESRC), e-Social Science Research Node *DReSS* (Grant Nº RES-149-25-0035, http://www.ncess.ac.uk/research/digital_records), and the ESRC e-Social Science small grants project *HeadTalk* (Grant Nº RES-149-25-1016). The discussion in Chapter 6 draws on the article 'Beyond the Word: New challenges in analysing corpora of spoken English' which has been previously published in the *European Journal of English Studies* 11(2). I am grateful to Ronald Carter and Dawn Knight for allowing me to use some of the material covered in this article for the purpose of this publication.

Most of the corpus examples in this book are taken from the Cambridge and Nottingham Corpus of Discourse in English (CANCODE). CANCODE is a 5-million-word computerised corpus of spoken English, made up of recordings from a variety of settings in the United Kingdom and Ireland. CANCODE was built by Cambridge University Press and the University of Nottingham and it forms part of the Cambridge International Corpus (CIC). Sole copyright of the corpus resides with Cambridge University Press, from whom all permissions to reproduce material must be obtained. I am grateful to Cambridge University Press for allowing me to include extracts, frequency lists and concordance data from the CANCODE corpus in this book.

List of tables and figures

Tables

Figures

CHAPTER 1

Introduction

1.0 Genesis of this book

The research for this publication draws on a number of spoken corpus resources with a view to gaining a better understanding of the extent to which the analysis of spoken corpus data might support the link between form and utterance function.

When pragmatic and functional theories of language and associated methods of analysis were first developed, the technology to capture and store large samples of spoken discourse in digital format was not yet available. This may be part of the reason for the emphasis on wider contextual and cognitive phenomena in the models that set out to explain how we do things with language. In the absence of spoken corpora which could be used to provide evidence for recurring links between form and function, a substantial proportion of pragmatic theories refer to phenomena that are external to the actual text and discourse in their explanation of utterance force and function.

With the development of spoken corpora of naturally occurring discourse and the accompanying tools required to represent and search this kind of data, it has become possible to re-examine the possible relationship between lexico-grammar, utterance function and discourse context, and to explore possible patterns in this relationship which are not external to the discourse, but which can be described through recurrence of choices at these three levels.

The past 10–15 years have seen the development of a number of spoken corpora, some of which are particularly concerned with representing language used in every-day life. They include the suite of spoken corpora collected at the University of Nottingham, such as the 5 million word Cambridge and Nottingham Corpus of Discourse in English (CANCODE) and, more recently, the Nottingham International Corpus of Learner English (NIC), as well as the Nottingham Health Communication Corpus (NHCC) and the Nottingham Multi-Modal Corpus (NMMC). The conversational data that have been collected as part of these corpus projects afford a new perspective on language function, as they provide the kind of evidence that has been largely missing from traditional theories developed in the area of pragmatics. It has thus become possible to re-investigate and re-evaluate some of the notions that have been developed in this area, such as the notion of the indirect speech act for example. The research presented in this book draws on these corpora to further explore the link between speech acts and lexico-grammar (see also Adolphs 2001).

When studying corpus data, the close relationship between linguistic form and utterance function becomes very obvious to the point where even very minor variations in form can be linked to a particular variable in the function of the utterance. This observation is, of course, not new and especially in the area of large scale corpus-based and corpus-driven lexicography, the relationship between form and meaning has been well-documented and theorised (see for example Sinclair 1996). Similarly, in the study of spoken discourse and utterance force, it has been shown that certain conversational routines, such as *Why don't you X* for example, can be linked to a particular speech act, in this case the speech act of suggestion (see Aijmer 1996).

However, the nature of the relationship between such 'conversational routines', as Aijmer calls them, and the context in which they are used, remains relatively under-explored. Yet, in order for us to be able to understand the extent to which conversational routines are 'primed' (Hoey 2005) to be used in a particular context and within a particular co-text, it is necessary to investigate whether there are any patterns within the text itself that can be linked to the use of a particular routine. Such patterns may be visible within the immediate lexico-grammatical environment of the routine or they may be evident within the wider discoursal context.

Other patterns might not be as easy to track due to the fact that a transcript of a conversation cannot offer a systematic and searchable record of the actual event. Corpus linguistic techniques are currently not able to track some of the key elements for the construction of meaning such as gesture and intonation for example. These are part of the immediate context, and they play an important role in the interpretation of utterances. Although technology to capture video and audio records of discourse events in natural settings is developing fast, the exploration of multi-modal corpora is still in its infancy. Yet, early research in this area suggests that we may have to go beyond the transcript to make sense of some of the regularities that exist between the choice of particular words or sequences of words and specific functions in discourse (see Knight et al. 2006). In order to explore the relationship between different channels of interacting in a discourse event, this book will also report on recent developments and analyses of multi-modal spoken corpora.

1.1 Overview

The main development of corpus linguistics as a methodology for language description has largely taken place in the area of lexicography, especially in relation to the ELT context, where patterns of usage of individual words or multi-word expressions are derived through the analysis of multi-million word corpora. Since such a focus requires a high degree of recurrence of the individual items that are being analysed, the size of the corpus resource has traditionally played a major part in achieving stable analytical results. As a consequence, the corpus resources that have informed this kind of research consist mainly of written language as this kind of variety is much easier to collect than spoken discourse, which has to undergo time and cost-intensive transcription before it can be subjected to corpus analysis.

There has thus been a noticeable focus on written language in the field and with written corpora now exceeding the one-billion-word mark, the possibilities for generating new insights into the way in which language is structured and used are both exciting and unprecedented. Spoken corpora, on the other hand, tend to be much smaller in size and thus unable to offer the same level of recurrence of individual items and phrases when compared to their written counterparts.

A further reason why the analysis of spoken discourse with the use of corpus-linguistic approaches has not received the same attention as the analysis of written discourse is because of the scepticism towards the applicability of corpus-based techniques to issues beyond the clause boundary (Conrad 2002:86). The analysis of discourse phenomena such as intonation, gesture or turn-taking for example requires different types of techniques compared to the study of lexico-grammar in a corpus as the units of analysis are not as clear-cut. Yet, those kinds of discourse level aspects of spoken interaction clearly form part of meaning construction and constitute one of the distinguishing features of spoken versus written discourse. It seems questionable then that the same techniques developed for written corpus analysis should be sufficient or appropriate for exploring spoken corpora, not least because discourse is an essentially collaborative event which is co-constructed by a number of participants in a discourse sequence where one contribution may directly influence the next. Given these issues, it would appear logical that when it comes to corpora of spoken discourse, the unit of analysis should be different to that of written discourse, although this is debatable and requires further exploration.

One of the aims of this book is to look more closely at the way in which smaller, spoken corpora might be analysed, not only in terms of lexico-grammatical patterns, but also in relation to issues which are at the heart of spoken discourse analysis, such as utterance function. This approach requires an investigation of a number of aspects of the discourse recorded in a spoken corpus. These include concordance level analysis and the description of co-textual patterns of selected words or phrases, as well as an analysis and grouping of contextual patterns which may be relevant in terms of a recurring match between form and function. The grouping and coding of contextual variables is an important step in this process and will be discussed in more detail throughout the book.

In order to explore further what a spoken corpus can offer in terms of describing and analysing utterance function, this book makes reference to four key areas of research: corpus linguistics, and more specifically the analysis of concordance outputs; pragmatics, with particular reference to utterance function and levels of directness; discourse analysis, with a focus on patterns and sequences in extended stretches of discourse; and context analysis, and the relationship between textual patterns and contextual variables. I argue that all four approaches are required to gain a better understanding of the scope of spoken corpus analysis in describing functional properties in spoken discourse, and that a combination of different approaches may assist us in the evaluation of specific concepts in each of the different areas.

To illustrate these points, and as outlined above, the book focuses on the description and extraction of functional properties of specific lexico-grammatical strings which have traditionally been associated with a particular speech act function, such as the string *Could you just* has been associated with the speech act of making a request. The book further explores the implications of using a spoken corpus in the analysis of speech act functions for some of the key notions within speech act theory, such as the distinction between a direct and an indirect speech act. In speech act theory, this distinction depends largely on the congruency of syntax and intended speech act function, i.e. on the match between sentence meaning and intended meaning, and on the use of modal items which may hedge the illocutionary force of an utterance. Following a corpus-based approach to analysing speech act function, this book considers whether the distinction between direct and indirect speech acts is useful and can be sustained, especially in the light of their association with wider social phenomena, such as politeness for example. In this context, it is argued that the notion of 'indirectness', as used in speech act theory, may have to be reconsidered and linked more explicitly to a larger discourse-based framework which takes account of the relationship between lexico-grammatical patterns and contextual variables as evidenced in language use.

One of the main questions that is explored in this book relates whether a pragmatic theory is necessary, or useful, when it comes to our understanding of utterance function, or whether a corpus-based analysis may provide a framework for describing such functions which relies mainly on a systematic extraction of text internal patterns. To deal with this question in some depth, the focus of the study has to be relatively narrow, and most of the chapters thus concentrate on one speech act function to exemplify the overall approach, that of making suggestions. In addition, the last chapter considers the function of signalling active listenership to illustrate the effect of working with multi-modal corpora in this field. While the use of backchannels in language is not a concern of traditional speech act theory, this area lends itself to illustrating the difference in scope when using spoken corpora that consist of transcripts only compared with multi-modal corpora. Signals of active listenership or 'backchannels' have an immediate gestural correlate, i.e. nods of the head, and the analysis of multi-modal corpora allows us to highlight the importance of the role of the listener in the way in which we may assess the utterance function expressed by the speaker.

1.2 Spoken discourse and corpus analysis

Following on from the early developments of relatively small sized spoken corpora in the 1960s, such as the London-Lund Corpus for example, the past two decades have seen major advances in the collection and development of spoken corpora, particularly in the English language but not exclusively. Some examples of spoken corpora are the Cambridge and Nottingham Corpus of Discourse in English *CANCODE* (McCarthy 1998), a five million word corpus collected mainly in Britain,[1] the Limerick Corpus of Irish English *LCIE* (Farr, Murphy and O'Keeffe 2004),[2] the Hong Kong Corpus of Spoken English *HKCSE* (see Cheng & Warren 1999, 2000, 2002),[3] the Michigan Corpus of Academic Spoken English *MICASE* (Simpson, Lucka & Ovens 2000),[4] and the Corpus of Spoken Professional American English *CSPAE*.[5] In addition, there is a growing interest in the development of spoken corpora of international varieties of English and other languages, as well as of learner language (e.g., Bolton et al. 2003; De Cock et al. 1998). These corpora provide researchers with rich samples of spoken language-in-use which form the basis of new and emerging descriptions of naturally occurring discourse.

Current research outputs based on the analysis of spoken corpora are wide-ranging and include, for example, descriptions of lexis and grammar (e.g. Biber et al. 1999; Carter & McCarthy 2006), discourse particles (Aijmer 2002), courtroom talk (Cotterill 2004), media discourse (O'Keeffe 2006) and health care communication (Adolphs et al. 2004). Current research in spoken corpus linguistics covers phenomena at utterance level, as well as at the level of discourse. A number of studies start with the exploration of concordance outputs and frequency information as a point of entry into the data and carry out subsequent analyses at the level of discourse (e.g. McCarthy 1998), while others start with a discourse analyt-

---

1.   www.cambridge.org/elt/corpus/cancode.htm

2.   www.ul.ie/~lcie/homepage.htm

3.   http://www.engl.polyu.edu.hk/department/academicstaff/Personal/ChengWinnie/HKCorpus_SpokenEnglish.htm

4.   http://micase.umdl.umich.edu/m/micase/

5.   www.athel.com/cpsa.html

ical approach followed by subsequent analyses of concordance data. There seems to be a common thread, then, in the research which uses spoken corpora, in that at least some consideration is given to the language that surrounds a particular word or sequence of words that goes beyond the span of +/– 4 at the concordance level. Recognition of the fact that spoken corpora are best analysed by using a combination of concordance level and discourse level description requires us to articulate clearly the relationship between the different frameworks that may be used to support such an approach.

The discourse level frameworks that may be relevant for the analysis of spoken corpora are not necessarily compatible with the kind of concordance-based and frequency driven analyses that are used in large scale lexicography studies. One of the key differences between spoken and written corpora is that most spoken discourse is collaborative in nature and as such it is more fluid and marked by emerging and changing orientations of the participants (McCarthy 1998). Yet, it is important to identify external categories for grouping transcripts in a corpus, especially where levels of formality and other functions are concerned which need to be judged against the wider context of the encounter. This process tends to be much more straightforward when dealing with written texts, as many of the genres that are used for written corpus analysis are well established, such as fiction versus non-fiction, letters versus e-mails etc. The group membership of such texts is more clearly demarcated than is the case with the majority of spoken discourse. The development of suitable frameworks for analysing spoken corpus data is thus particularly complex and further research is needed to assess whether the analysis of concordance data and discourse phenomena can ever be fully integrated.

1.3 Pragmatics and corpus evidence

The systematic exploration of utterance function has been a key concern in the area of pragmatics. One of the general assumptions in pragmatics is that the interpretation of language in use is based in part on the meaning of the actual words that are being used and in part on other sources of knowledge, including knowledge about contextual and cultural norms. As such pragmatic theories do not assume a one to one relationship between language form and utterance function, but instead are concerned with accounting for the processes that give rise to a particular interpretation of an utterance that is used in a particular context.

In doing so, a range of different methods and approaches have been developed which come under the very broad heading of Pragmatics. Spencer-Oatey and Ze-garac (2002:84) distinguish between the cognitive-psychological approach which is marked by the analysis and discussion of decontextualised utterances and their possible interpretations, and the social-psychological approach. The latter tends 'to focus on the ways in which particular communicative exchanges between individuals are embedded in and constrained by social, cultural and other contextual factors' (ibid).

Depending on which perspective is taken, the methods that are being used to explain the relationship between 'signs' and 'users' vary. They range from philosophical explorations of the 'conditions' that have to be met for the achievement of a particular interpretation of a message to corpus-based explorations of recurrent matches between particular forms and functions (see DeClerck 2004), to the use of discourse completion tasks, detailed field notes and interviews relating to a particular communicative event and/or function.

Yet, the majority of research within the area of pragmatics has not used attested examples of language-in-use and has not been directly concerned with understanding the relationship between language form and function. One of the key philosophical traditions that shaped pragmatics is Speech Act Theory, first advanced by Austin and Searle in the 1960s. This theory coincided with the development of a number of positions which argued for the disparity between 'langue' and 'parole' (Saussure 1916 [1966]) and 'competence' and 'performance' (Chomsky 1965) and emphasised the importance of studying language competence rather than language-in-use. Since it is impossible to extract a possible correlation between language form and function without considering language-in-use, the focus within the area of pragmatics has been mainly on the description of the processes and conditions that have to be met for an utterance to be interpreted as carrying a particular function (see Levinson 1983; Leech 1983 for a discussion). The area of pragmatics has traditionally relied on invented examples to illustrate such conditions. Stubbs (1996: 200) argues in this context that

> Searle's (1969, 1979) systematization of Austin is much more rigid, and moves even further away from actual language behaviour, leaving speech act theory in the odd position of demanding a study of language in social action within a theory of social institutions [...], but studying almost nothing but invented data.

Stubbs (ibid) proposes to use a corpus to study the use of illocutionary verbs which will lead to a better understanding of their status within a broader theory of speech action. However, illocutionary verbs are not the only category which would benefit from close corpus analysis. One of the issues which has received substantial attention within pragmatics, including in more empirically-based studies in this area, is the notion of indirectness and the associated concept of the indirect speech act. The level of indirectness in this tradition has been closely linked to contextual factors but has not yet been fully explored with reference to corpus data. A corpus-based analysis of lexical items and formulae which marks indirectness would provide the evidence needed for a discussion about the relationship between form and function in terms of speech acts.

Corpus research has resulted in a general shift in focus from the disparity between form and function to a description of lexical items that is based to a large
extent on recurring patterns in language-in-use (Stubbs 1995, 1996; Sinclair 1991,
1996). There is a considerable amount of corpus research which illustrates the relationship between form and function of individual lexical items and multi-word
units (e.g. DeBeaugrande 1996; Sinclair 1991, 1996; Stubbs 1995, 1996). Sinclair
(1996) outlines a methodology for analysing the 'units of meaning' of individual
words and multi-word strings using corpus resources. He illustrates that the meaning of a lexical item includes such aspects as the habitual co-occurrence with other
words (collocation), grammatical integration, as well as the 'semantic prosody'
(Louw 1993) which 'expresses something close to the 'function' of the item' (Sinclair 1996: 87). Stubbs (1995) shows, for example, how the word *cause* has acquired
a negative semantic prosody and thus, when chosen, implies a functional choice,
as well as a semantic choice.

1.4 Speech act expressions

As far as the study of utterance function is concerned, the kinds of approach developed by Sinclair (1996, 2004), Stubbs (1995) and Hoey (2005) suggest that the
analysis of corpus evidence should allow us to arrive at a much more accurate description, and thus understanding, of the relationship between recurrent linguistic
forms and their function in discourse.

The existence of recurrent matches between linguistic form and speech act
function is well-documented and theorised (Levinson 1983; Austin 1962; Sadock
1974; Aijmer 1996). In the area of language pedagogy, 'lexical frames' have been
widely discussed (Pawley & Syder 1983; Nattinger & DeCarrico 1992). The use
of 'lists' of certain speech act expressions which realise a particular function has a
long-standing tradition in English language teaching textbooks and grammars (see
for example Leech & Svartvik 1994; Dörnyei & Thurrell 1992). Often, such lists are
accompanied by suggestions to the learner as to which expression is judged to be
more polite in comparison with others (e.g. Leech & Svartvik 1994: 168).

Theories concerned with the level of directness of individual forms and syntactic structures have been advanced by Brown and Levinson (1987) and Leech
(1983) who have related linguistic levels of indirectness to the notion of 'cost' or
'imposition' on the hearer, as well as to the relationship between the speakers. And
while these theories are based on observations of language-in-use to a certain extent, the exact relationship between 'indirect' speech acts and their meaning in
context has yet to be analysed in a systematic, corpus-based way.

Empirical studies of utterance function are prominent in the field of cross-
linguistic enquiry, where differences between native and non-native speaker be-

haviour are being analysed (see for example Olshtain 1983, 1989; Garcia 1989; House & Kasper 1981; House 1989; Manes & Wolfson 1981; Coulmas 1981). A large part of the work on speech act expressions in this area has relied on Discourse Completion Tasks (DCTs) or similar elicitation formats (e.g. Blum-Kulka 1982; House & Kasper 1987; Blum-Kulka; House & Kasper 1989; Barron 2003). As yet it is not clear how the different methods in the pragmatics toolkit compare and whether the growing development of international spoken corpora might be a useful resource for investigations in cross-cultural pragmatics.

Aijmer (1996) carries out a pioneering corpus-based study of conversational routines in English using the London-Lund Corpus. She develops a classification of the various conversational routines in discourse according to their degree of fixedness, institutionalisation, situational dependence and syntactic form (1996: 1). Her main organising principles are speech acts. She discusses thanking, apologies, requests and offers in terms of their routinised 'function indicating devices'. She covers speech acts that have received a lot of attention in the discussion of conversational routines (Eisenstein & Bodman 1986; Goffman 1967; Levinson 1983). Aijmer's account lists all of the linguistic forms in the corpus that realise a certain speech act rather than studying the 'unit of meaning' of individual speech act expressions.

One of the main obstacles in analysing utterance function using a corpus-based approach is that we can search a corpus only for language forms, not for functions. As Swales (http://www.lsa.umich.edu/eli/micase/How_to_function .htm) points out

> Starting with a lexical item [...] is relatively straightforward, at least initially, because one can be fairly sure of capturing all the tokens [...]. Starting with a functional category, in contrast, means searching the grammatical and pragmatic literature as well as racking one's brains in order to come up with a list of possible realizations.

This means that the initial choice of the kinds of speech act expressions to be analysed has to be made by the researcher. As a consequence, the focus of the analysis has to be on the patterns that emerge from the use of specific realisations, the identification of which is partly based on intuition. While this is not necessarily a limiting factor, it does delineate the extent to which corpus analysis can inform pragmatic theories in that the focus of a corpus enquiry has to start with the form and not the function. As a result, it may not be possible to develop an all encompassing framework of 'conditions' that would lead to specific functional interpretations of utterances. However, a corpus approach does allow for a re-examination of the status assigned to such conditions in discourse-in-use. That is, the patterns of usage of individual lexical items and phrases may point to a theory of understanding meaning and function which is much more textual than previously argued.

In addition, corpora collected from different contexts allow for an analysis of the distribution of such items and phrases that are tightly associated with particular functions in language. This in turn makes it possible to examine claims about the relationship between context and the interpretation of functions more rigorously and more empirically. The analysis of distributions of such items across different contexts further allows for a discussion of the relationship between text and context, and of the status and saliency of different elements within the two that define this relationship.

A corpus-based analysis of pragmatic properties thus allows for a re-evaluation of the distinction between semantics and pragmatics. Many of the elements that have traditionally been dealt with through pragmatic frameworks, such as issues of politeness and indirectness, could be discussed in terms of their recurrence and patterns in relation to individual lexical items and phrases. We may find that when speech act expressions are studied on the basis of corpus data much of the discussion about inference procedures and felicity conditions becomes secondary or altogether unnecessary. Instead, it should be possible to establish functional profiles of a number of speech act expressions which are based on the distributional and collocational patterns in use.

1.5 Corpus and context

In order to develop such functional profiles, we need to be able to make explicit the relationship between individual speech act expressions and their distribution across different contexts. The view that context is closely related to text and discourse is adopted in a range of traditions, including conversation analysis (CA) and systemic functional linguistics (SFL). Hasan (1999: 224), for example, argues

> that to describe the nature of human language we need to place it in its social environment; that this environment – call it context – must be taken as an integral part of linguistic theory; that the linguistic theory is stratal, consisting of four strata: context, semantics, lexico-grammar and phonology. These represent four distinct orders of abstraction, which are both necessary and sufficient for a satisfactory description of language.

In terms of pragmatic theories, there has been a general division between lexico-grammar and context and, as a result, the close analysis of individual lexical items and phrases in terms of their relationship with contextual and pragmatic properties has received little attention. Thibault and van Leeuwen take this view as their point of departure in a paper which argues for the direct relationship between lexico-grammar and context:

> The division of language into syntax, semantics, and pragmatics is widely accepted. In this view, speech acts cannot be specified on the basis of lexico-grammatical criteria. Instead, they belong in a separate 'pragmatics' of utterances in their contexts-of-use. (1996:561)

Corpus evidence should be able to shed some light on the relationship between lexico-grammar and context and, in doing so, provide a basis for renewed discussion about the extent to which text-external elements are invoked in our interpretations of utterances. However, this approach would be different to previous work which has discussed the link between syntax and function, and which has resulted in the coining of the notion 'indirect speech act'. Levinson (1983:242) explores the relationship between sentence types (i.e. interrogative, imperative and declarative) and illocution (i.e. questioning, ordering and stating). However, the fact that there are many utterances where this relationship cannot be demonstrated reinforces the premise that utterance force is 'pragmatic' and not directly correlated with syntax. Instances where the grammatical form differs from its functional correlate are examples of 'indirect speech acts'. Examples of incongruent syntax and speech act function are often discussed in terms of contextual criteria and with reference to theories of politeness (see Brown & Levinson 1987).

In a corpus-based approach, there is no need for the distinction between direct and indirect speech acts outlined above. The starting point is the speech act expression rather than the sentence mood, and functional properties of the speech act expression are investigated in terms of the patterns that emerge both at the concordance level and at the level of discourse. In terms of the distribution of individual speech act expressions, a corpus-based approach also allows for a more empirically based description of linguistic choices according to culturally recognised discourse groupings. But how do we know that the contextual categories applied in the design of a corpus are relevant?

With corpus design becoming an increasingly important part of the corpus research process, a considerable effort is dedicated to the selection and groupings of texts, spoken and written, that make up any one corpus. Corpus design thus involves demarcating particular contexts that are widely recognised. Different contextual coding schemes have been developed and applied to different corpora over the years. The CANCODE corpus, for example, is categorised according to the relationship that holds between the speakers and the type of activity that the speakers are engaged in, while MICASE uses a different categorisation scheme which includes, for example, the type of academic activity that takes place at the time of recording, e.g. tutorials, lectures etc. Corpus design takes account of the notion of context and in doing so corpus designers refer to recognised 'schemas' (Cook 1994) or 'frames' (Aijmer 1996).

However, designs of contextual categories for constructing spoken corpora can be ad-hoc and often relate directly to the particular research aim that the corpus resource is built to address. Further reference to research into the description and analysis of discourse contexts is thus a pre-requisite for any study that tries to relate textual patterns to contextual categories.

The notion of context has been discussed widely in different research traditions. Christie (1986:222) discusses context in terms of a 'culturally significant way of meaning' while others use the term 'genre' to describe the different dimensions of context (Swales 1990; Bakhtin 1986). Genres, or 'generically-oriented activity' (McCarthy 1998:46) have been described both in terms of text structure (Ventola 1987; Hasan 1985) and according to participants' goals in discourse (McCarthy 1998; Dudley-Evans 1994; Tracy & Coupland 1990).

In his study of CANCODE data, McCarthy (1998) finds recurrent linguistic features that are tied to certain types of goal-orientation in discourse. This observation would suggest that the meaning of speech act expressions may also contain information about the particular genre in which they occur most frequently. Further support for this idea can be derived from Halliday's (1985:37) observation that the lexical string *once upon a time* conjures up associations of story-telling genres. While a number of theoretical frameworks exist that outline the relationship between semantic features and 'genre' (Hasan 1985; Halliday 1985; Longacre 1983; Biber 1989), none of them focus directly on speech act expressions and goal-types in discourse. This book thus aims to address the relationship between theories of text and context and their relevance to the exploration of speech act expressions, using a spoken corpus as the basis for discussion.

Aijmer (1996:26) argues that 'all routines are to some extent constrained by the situation. They can be restricted with regard to the antecedent event, the setting, the participants in the conversation, etc'. Levinson (1983), in a discussion of speech acts in context, uses the term 'frame' as a possible analytical notion to capture the intricate relationship between individual speech acts and the environment in which they occur. A frame, Levinson (1983:281) points out,

> is a body of knowledge that is evoked in order to provide an inferential base for the understanding of an utterance [...] and we may suggest that in the attribution of force or function [...] reference is made, as relevant, to the frames for teaching, shopping, participating in committee meetings, lecturing and other speech events (see e.g. Gumperz 1977).

Linguistic choices are thus influenced by the way in which speakers orient themselves to a 'higher-order framework' (McCarthy 1998). This includes knowledge about certain contexts and the restrictions and constraints that such contexts pose on possible contributions, as well as the structural progression of discourse (see Brown and Yule (1983) for a discussion). This particular issue is at the heart of the study of 'genre' (see for example Hammond & Derewianka 2001). The power of the concept 'genre' lies in 'the attractiveness of its potential to formalise generic aspects of the structure of texts [...]' (Knapp 1997: 113). Genre theory, then, is based on the 'view that texts can be classifiable and have understandable and predictable forms, structures and purposes' (ibid).

However, while from a corpus-design point of view it might be possible to find groupings for texts that are based loosely on a recognised speech event, most spoken interactions are highly dynamic in nature, and participants may change the way in which they invoke the contextual norms at any point during the interaction. We should therefore not expect a straightforward relationship between speech act expressions and context, however this is defined. Yet, this does not mean that context can be ignored in a corpus-based description, but rather that emerging analytical results need to be discussed against the backdrop of the dynamic processes involved in naturally occurring interaction.

1.5.1 Discourse Context

Apart from the wider context of the situation in which individual speech act expressions are used, there is a further layer of context which is concerned mainly with the local discourse-level negotiation of meaning. Traditional pragmatic theory has focused mainly on utterances as the unit of analysis and, as a result, the relationship between discourse co-text and utterance force has not been fully explored in such frameworks. The description of levels of indirectness becomes difficult when the discourse co-text is not fully taken into account, as the placement of utterances contributes significantly to their meaning and function. The kind of ambiguity that has concerned speech act theorists, i.e. the way in which we might be able to explain why an utterance in the interrogative mood might not be functioning as a question, but maybe as an order, does not seem to be a problem when we look at actual examples in context (see also Sinclair 1992; Tsui 1994).

Line		
1	\<S03\>	They're all sitting there with their skirts \<$E\> laughs \</$E\> up to about there.
2	\<S01\>	\<$=\> Nancy's Nancy's mother \</$=\> Nancy is+
3	\<S03\>	Unbelievable.
4	\<S01\>	+forever telling her mother to pull her skirt up.
5	\<S02\>	I do. Bloody thing.
6	\<S01\>	And saying **Why don't you wear longer skirts**. And Nancy's mother says Ooh
7		I canna do that \<$G?\>.
8	\<S04\>	How old she then?
9	\<S01\>	Seventy eight. Isn't she.

The following extract from CANCODE illustrates this point (please see appendix for transcription conventions).

In this short extract we find four speakers chatting on the topic of clothes, and the appropriate length of skirts in particular. In line 6, speaker 1 (<S01>) reports a suggestion: *Why don't you wear longer skirts*. Suggestions are particularly interesting with regard to the interface of semantic and pragmatic properties and are not easily described in terms of current speech act taxonomies. They have been treated as 'sub-acts' of 'directives' (Searle 1969; Tsui 1994) or 'requestives'(Tsui 1994) and have not received much attention as a speech act category in their own right. The kinds of speech act expressions that often realise suggestions illustrate the issues surrounding direct and indirect speech acts. In a non-reported structure, an utterance such as the one above could be a question or a suggestion depending on the context in which it is used, i.e. whether it is based on syntactic structure or on conventionalised associations (Sadock 1974).

Apart from the prominent role played by the phenomenon of conventionalised association, there are a number of factors which are intrinsic in the discourse stretch in the example above, and which make the suggestive function more likely than the questioning function, albeit in the reported structure. These include the previous negative evaluation *with their skirts up to about there*, a string of other negative evaluative expressions by different speakers *unbelievable, bloody thing*, and also the reported response to the suggestion *Ooh I canna do that*. This kind of response appears to address an order/suggestion rather than answer a question such as the one used in line 8 for example. A closer look at the discourse episode which includes this particular suggestion shows that in order to disambiguate the speech act, it may not be necessary to resort to complex inference processes that rely on wider contextual knowledge.

While the focus on speech act expressions is used in this volume to describe patterns of co-occurrence of illocutionary force, lexico-grammar and context in a spoken corpus, the relationship between these elements has previously been discussed with reference to indirect speech acts which are not conventionally indirect. Thibault and van Leeuwen (1996) draw on the following example from Searle's (1975:61) work on indirect speech acts:

> Student X: Let's go to the movies tonight.
> Student Y: I have to study for an exam.

While this example does not include a speech act expression which might tie it to a particular function, they claim that it is unnecessary to refer to inference rules to describe how the utterance by student Y should be interpreted. Instead, they argue that 'X simply knows that mentioning another incompatible activity is a conventional way of realising the speech act of 'turning down an invitation', signifying that he or she should not interpret the response as a complete rejection' (1996:565).

This argument is akin to the idea that recurrent ways of expressing a particular function could lead to them being closely associated with such a function to the point where no inference procedures are necessary. However, it is difficult to see how such a view might be supported through the analysis of corpus data, given the range of possible paradigmatic options that might realise a particular function.

When we start with the speech act expression, on the other hand, we may be able to expand on the position developed by Thibault and van Leeuwen by studying the correlation between form, function and context in an empirical manner. In doing so, it is important that the wider discourse context beyond the single utterance is taken into account. Once we move beyond the concordance line, there are, of course, other issues that need to be considered, such as the extent of the unit of analysis. This is an area which has received much attention in different traditions that deal with spoken discourse analysis. In narrowing down the initial starting point of the analysis to a specific speech act expression, we can develop a 'bottom-up' approach to explore any emerging patterns and assess how far they extend into the on-going discourse. As such, a corpus-based approach can offer a point of entry into a multi-level analysis which includes collocational patterns of the speech act expression, discourse-level patterns of the types of utterances that precede and succeed the speech act expression, as well as wider contextual patterns that can be analysed in terms of distributional frequencies across genres and text-types, and across socio-demographic variables pertaining to the speakers who use the expressions.

1.6 Why this book?

Corpus-based research into utterance function is a relatively under-explored area at present, despite the fact that a number of key journals in the area of pragmatics now feature corpus-based research, including, for example, a special issue on corpus linguistics in the *Journal of Pragmatics* in 2004. Difficulties associated with assembling and analysing spoken corpora and the inevitable focus on lexical rather than functional units and concordance lines rather than extended discourse stretches in corpus research have all led to a general scepticism of corpus exploration as a useful approach to study pragmatic functions. In addition, the fact that spoken language is multi-modal in nature and that meaning is created through an interplay of a range of semiotic modalities contributes further to the unease that often accompanies this particular line of enquiry.

However, despite the reluctant uptake of corpus-based techniques in studying pragmatic functions, it seems that corpus linguistics has a lot to offer to pragmatics as a discipline and vice versa (O'Keeffe 2007). Spoken corpora can provide researchers in the area of pragmatics with attested examples of language in use while pragmatics can offer frameworks for interpreting patterns of use that go beyond the level of lexico-grammar.

This book aims to explore further the relationship between corpus linguistics and pragmatics by developing a new approach to the analysis of utterance function that is based on spoken corpus data. This involves close consideration of the unit of analysis, including the different strata of discourse that form part of meaning generation. The main focus is on articulating the kinds of patterns at the different levels of discourse that support stronger reliance on text-internal criteria for the description and understanding of meaning in interaction. Individual speech act expressions that have strong associations with particular utterance functions are used as the starting point for the different explorations. While the main part of this book draws on transcripts of conversations, Chapter 6 discusses the analysis of multi-modal corpora and the consequences of extending the unit of analysis to include a set of gestural elements.

1.7 Organisation of this book

The book is divided into seven chapters and progresses from an introductory overview of spoken corpus analysis and associated methodologies to a more specific discussion of utterance function in context. The data that form the basis of this discussion includes both transcript-only corpora and multi-modal corpora.

In terms of individual chapters, following the general overview and outline of this book provided in the present chapter, Chapter 2 considers in more detail the issues of spoken corpus analysis, and how a more quantitative approach might be combined with discourse-level investigation. Chapter 2 also discusses different approaches towards the analysis of meaning in interaction with a focus on the relationship between semantics and pragmatics. The differences between spoken corpus analysis and other methods in studying utterance function will also be explored.

Drawing on data from the CANCODE corpus, Chapter 3 discusses the role of collocation and co-text of individual speech act expressions for the purpose of functional disambiguation, for example in deciding whether a phrase introduces a question or suggestion. The development of functional profiles for speech act expressions is proposed in this chapter which includes the notion of functional prosodies.

Chapter 4 deals with the issue of context in relation to utterance function. The chapter discusses the way in which the relationship between text and context has been conceptualised in the past, and explores the role of corpus data in this discussion. Corpora are principled collections of texts and the principles on which their design is based are often directly related to culturally recognised contexts.

This chapter draws on corpus data to establish the link between lexico-grammar and context in relation to speech act expressions. Possible motivations for indirectness such as considerations of politeness for example, are discussed in relation to contextual constraints that are reflected in particular patterns of indirectness in language-in-use. It is argued that patterns of indirectness are describable in terms of their distribution across different contexts. Existing frameworks which link power, speaker relationship and the rate of the imposition to levels of linguistic directness, as proposed by Brown and Levinson (1983) for example, are discussed in the light of actual variation across contexts in spoken corpora.

Chapter 5 extends this analysis to the discourse co-text of individual speech act expressions. The role of discoursal patterns in the description of functional profiles of speech act expressions is the focus of this chapter. The notion of the discourse episode is advanced as a possible unit of analysis to aid the description of directness and meaning potential of individual utterances. The discourse episode reflects the dynamic nature of discourse in that it takes account of emerging goal-orientation and goal negotiation of participants. As such, it includes utterances beyond the traditional dyad which might contribute to the interpretation of a specific speech act expression.

There are a number of layers in face-to-face interaction which contribute to the meaning of an utterance. While research on spoken corpora so far has mainly focused on analysing transcripts, new developments in the compilation of corpora with aligned data-streams, including text, sound and video, afford new descriptions of how these different modalities interact to create meaning in discourse. Chapter 6 explores the impact of multi-modal corpus analysis on investigations of utterance function. The role of patterns at the level of gesture is discussed in relation to descriptive and applied issues pertinent to spoken corpus analysis.

The book ends with a summary of the main points that emerge from the research reported in the different chapters and a discussion of the issues which might be addressed as spoken corpus analysis develops further.

CHAPTER 2

Spoken discourse and corpus analysis

2.0 Introduction

Over the last twenty years or so, corpus-based research has received much attention not only in the field of lexical studies (Sinclair 1991; Stubbs 2001), but also in the area of grammar research (Biber et al. 1999; Carter & McCarthy 2006) and empirical pragmatic investigations (Aijmer 1996; Svartvik 1980). In the field of grammar research, the analysis of spoken corpora show new syntactic patterns that have been marginalised in the past (see Carter & McCarthy 2006). Furthermore, the level of description that becomes possible with carefully annotated spoken corpora allows for a more socially informed grammar where the level of formality can be taken into account. Carter and McCarthy (1995) find for example that the *going to* future is often used in more informal situations than the *will* future.

The development of corpus linguistics in the 1960s and 1970s has coincided with a growing interest in the study and description of pragmatic functions in spoken interaction (see Kennedy 1998: 174). Svartvik's (1980) study of discourse particles in the London-Lund Corpus, and Aijmer's (1984, 1986) and Stenström's (1990) work on hedging devices all illustrate how spoken corpora can help generate new insights into pragmatic functions in use. In 1975 Sinclair and Coulthard developed a framework for studying discourse with the use of real data recorded initially in classroom settings. Corpus linguistic approaches and discourse analysis have since often been used as complementary frameworks in the description of spoken language (see Leech 2000 for a discussion). The new emphasis on studying language-in-use, and the implications for the description of pragmatic functions, have affected the way in which we conceptualise the relationship between form and function in language.

In speech act theory in particular, the use of invented examples has supported a division between form and function, as discussed in the previous chapter. Rather than concentrating on patterns in language use, traditional speech act theory has focused on finding ways to explain the disparity between linguistic form and meaning in context. Corpus-based analyses of speech acts in use, on the other hand, illustrate that the form-function division might not be borne out in corpus data and cannot be sustained as the main focus of pragmatic investigations. Aijmer (1996), for example, carries out a study of routinised speech act expressions in the

London-Lund Corpus and her study illustrates that a close analysis of such expressions allows a level of linguistic description which includes patterns of speech act function in relation to form.

This chapter considers in more detail the issue of using corpus data and methods of representing this kind of data to analyse and describe functions in spoken discourse. This includes practical issues of representing conversation through an orthographic transcript, as well as theoretical issues of studying functions in relation to frequency and distribution of lexical items and speech act expressions. The chapter starts with a brief overview of how language function has traditionally been approached and conceived of within linguistics. The notion of function in language is conceptualised in different ways in the wide range of linguistic traditions that deal with this issue. The chapter therefore includes a brief overview of the 'pragmatics toolkit' and considers different approaches to analysing language function in spoken discourse. This discussion generates some key questions about the integrity of orthographic transcripts when they are used as the basis for linguistic description. Transcription issues are discussed in relation to some of the key questions surrounding corpus design, data collection and representation. The chapter further considers the role of context and how contextual categories implicated in the process of corpus design might be exploited to study the relationship between linguistic choice and context in an empirical manner.

2.1   Language as data

The previous chapter has already briefly touched upon the issue of the nature of evidence that is being used to advance language description and language theory. When language takes on the status of data to inform research questions and procedures, the kind of language that we draw on is of major importance and often becomes part of the research paradigm itself. A very broad distinction between language-in-use and language-as-abstract is often made with reference to scholars like Chomsky and Saussure who have established distinct categories of 'competence' and 'performance' (Chomsky 1965) and 'langue' and 'parole' (Saussure 1916 [1966]). This distinction which is broadly in line with the distinction between empiricist and rationalist approaches to data gathering and analysis has been discussed extensively in relation to corpus linguistics (see for example McEnery & Wilson 2001: 5–16 and Stubbs 1996 Chapter 2). This is partly due to the fact that corpus linguistics emerged at a similar time as Chomskyan theories in the 1960s, and partly because corpus linguistics is firmly defined by its focus on language-in-use which puts it at opposite ends with more rationalist approaches in which language is seen as a cognitive phenomenon.

The results of large-scale corpus research have allowed for a reassessment of Chomskyan theories of language, especially in relation to the status assigned to meaning and grammar (see Sinclair 2004, chapter 8). While Chomsky viewed the two as independent, corpus studies illustrate that in language-in-use they are interrelated and that a difference in form will be reflected in a difference in meaning (see Stubbs 1996:36–41 for a discussion). Furthermore, the dualism between 'langue' and 'parole' set up by Saussure, has been criticised by corpus linguists (see, for example, Sinclair 1991). Large-scale corpus investigations provide the kind of data that allows a different approach to the way in which we conceptualise 'language-in-use' and 'language-as-abstract' in that patterns in language use determine, and are determined by, the different possibilities of structuring language. As a consequence, the distinction between what can be observed and what is possible becomes unnecessary.

The different positions that have been articulated in relation to the kind of language evidence on which our descriptions and theories are based are of considerable relevance to pragmatic investigations. As outlined in the introductory chapter, despite a clear concern with language-in-use, much of the work in pragmatics has been based on invented examples of utterances based on native speaker intuition. The overall aim has been to describe the potential ambiguities that might prevent hearers from understanding the intended meaning, and to define sets of rules and conditions that speakers and hearers may attend to when faced with such ambiguities. Yet, when we study actual language-in-use as represented in a corpus, many of the ambiguities disappear. For example, the ambiguity of the verb *can*, which is often cited in the traditional speech act theory literature as an item which may introduce a question or a request, may not be an issue if a large sample of concordance lines is consulted and its prototypical meaning emerges through an analysis of lexico-grammatical patterns. Sinclair (1996 [2004]) illustrates how corpus analysis of units of meaning addresses some of the kinds of issues that a word-based description cannot easily handle. He argues that 'some of the problems of conventional description are much reduced – for example there will be little word-based ambiguity left when this model has been applied thoroughly' (1996 [2004]:40).

De Beaugrande (1996:504) also critiques the use of invented data as the basis for linguistic theories. He draws attention to a number of data handling strategies employed by the non-empiricist linguist, such as 'rarefying' (taking out markers of interpersonality), 'decontextualising' (treating utterances in isolation, out of their context), 'introspecting' (making intuitive estimations about data samples and deciding which ones are grammatical and which ones are not), 'collating', 'generalising' and 'consulting informants'. These strategies have furthered certain preconceptions about language, especially in relation to the division between form and meaning, form and function and competence and performance.

Corpus-based investigations of language functions are therefore well placed to address some of the issues that are at the heart of speech act theory, such as the notion of 'indirectness'. In addition, a spoken corpus can provide evidence for the study of discourse-based phenomena which speech act theory has not concerned itself with, such as false starts, incomplete utterances, interruptions and backchannels, but which nevertheless carry important functional information. With a main focus on philosophical issues, speech act theory has not explored the potential value of spoken corpora in helping to address some of its key concerns.

There are other areas of pragmatics which have traditionally been more open to the idea of using performance data, including various social-psychological approaches (Spencer-Oatey & Zegarac 2002: 84). Studies of interlanguage pragmatics, in particular, require an analysis of patterns of language-in-use. However, the approach to data in such studies does not usually involve close corpus analysis but rather the use of Discourse Completion Tasks (DCTs) or role play enacted by native speakers (see, for example, House & Kasper 1981, 1987; Eisenstein & Bodman 1986; Barron 2003).

The extent to which DCT data is different to corpus data has not been explored sufficiently to assess the value of the different approaches in relation to data description. And language description for its own sake is arguably not the focus of cross-linguistic studies. However, as Schauer and Adolphs (2006) illustrate in a study of expressions of gratitude in DCT data versus corpus data, the fact that data generated through DCTs is based around single utterances distorts the overall picture of a speech act which is often negotiated and developed over a number of turns in a dynamic discourse event. It is therefore unclear whether DCT or role play data display the same patterns and attributes as naturally occurring data stored in a spoken corpus. The advances made in the field of cross-linguistic research in relation to analysing language function thus need to be assessed alongside corpus-based descriptions of such functions in order to gain a better understanding of the impact and value of using different data-sets to address a variety of concerns in the area of pragmatics.

2.2 Language functions

The notion of *function* in language plays a major role in a number of different traditions in linguistic analysis and description. However, there is no clear-cut definition that is universally accepted. Instead, we find that the term is being used to describe different phenomena which are tied to varying degrees to actual language-in-use. *Syntactic functions*, for example, refer to the role of subject, object etc. in a phrase, and *macro-functions* refer broadly to the role that language plays as part of a speaker's experience (see Bühler 1934; Jakobson 1960; Malinowski 1923;

Firth 1957 and Halliday 1973, 1978). Halliday (1970) distinguishes between the ideational, interpersonal and the textual function. The *ideational function* refers to the expression of content while the *interpersonal function* serves to establish and maintain social relations, and the *textual function* relates to the construction of text in context. These *macro-functions* relate directly to the organisation of language and are reflected in linguistic choices made by the speaker.

Within speech act theory the term *function* refers mainly to the notion of *illocutionary force* (Austin 1962; Searle 1969, 1971). Austin (1962) divided utterances into three components, the *locution*, *illocution* and *perlocution*, a division that is broadly akin to the macro-functions proposed by Halliday. This division allows for a distinction between the linguistic form, which is conveyed through declarative, interrogative and imperative sentence mood and the function which utterances carry in a specific situation.

The overall division into macro-functions reinforces the division between form and function of speech acts and reflects the general direction in which speech act theory has moved since it was first developed. The way in which the different macro-functions interact with one another, especially in terms of the nature of the relationship between linguistic form and function, has remained relatively under-explored. It is this area where a spoken corpus may offer the kind of evidence which would allow the study of linguistic patterns in relation to patterns in speech act function. This approach will be explored further in the next section.

2.3 Pragmatics and corpus linguistics

The theoretical premise at the heart of speech act theory assumes that utterances in language use perform certain actions and that those utterances can be understood by means of reference to the context in which they occur. In order to develop better descriptions of what such a context might consist of and look like, a corpus might be a useful resource. However, while a focus on performance data is a main feature of corpus linguistics (see Biber et al. 1998:4), speech act theory has not made use of such kind of data to explicate context. The question that arises is thus whether corpus linguistics merely offers an empirical data resource for pragmatic investigations or whether there are key differences in underlying assumptions. In order to address this question, it is necessary to examine the remit of pragmatics in more detail. As outlined above, the area of pragmatics is relatively difficult to define as the boundaries can become blurred with other areas, such as discourse analysis and sociolinguistics, for example. This is because many other linguistic disciplines are concerned with the interpretation of utterances. Levinson (1983:5) points out in this context:

This diversity of possible definitions and lack of clear boundaries may be disconcerting, but it is by no means unusual: since academic fields are congeries of preferred methods, implicit assumptions, and focal problems or subject matters, attempts to define them are rarely wholly satisfactory.

While it may be difficult to define the area of pragmatics in more general terms, it is possible to outline the main differences between pragmatic theories and corpus linguistics, concentrating on preferred methods and implicit assumptions.

The main difference between the two approaches lies in the way in which 'meaning' is conceptualised. Pragmatics is often contrasted with semantics in that pragmatics is concerned with any features which are non-semantic and related to context. Variation in linguistic structure or grammar which are due to semantic variation, thus fall into the area of pragmatics. This distinction does, of course, assume that function and meaning can be separated in the first place. Corpus linguistics takes a different view of meaning and form. Sinclair (1991) points out that there is no distinction between form and meaning, and that the two are inseparable, just as lexis and grammar are interdependent. Language function thus becomes part of the unit of meaning of a lexical item which also includes information about its grammatical integration, collocations and semantic preference (see Sinclair [1996] 2004). Sinclair argues in this context:

> A semantic prosody (Louw 1993) is attitudinal, and on the pragmatic side of the semantics/pragmatics continuum. It is thus capable of a wide range of realisation, because in pragmatic expressions the normal semantic values of the words are not necessarily relevant. But once noticed among the variety of expression, it is immediately clear that the semantic prosody has a leading role to play in the integration of an item with its surroundings. It expresses something close to the 'function' of the items – it shows how the rest of the item is to be interpreted functionally.
>
> (Sinclair 2004: 34)

If we assume that meaning exists on a continuum between semantics and pragmatics and that meaning can be described on the basis of recurrent patterns in a corpus, then we should be able to extract functional information from such recurrent uses as well.

The difference between pragmatics and corpus linguistics is thus not merely based on the data that informs the theory. Instead, both disciplines are based on different assumptions in relation to meaning and have therefore established different methods of describing language. The next section will look at the interface between speech act theory and corpus linguistics in more detail.

2.4 Speech Act Theory and corpus linguistics

Speech Act Theory emerged in the 1960s with the work of the English philosopher John Austin and was later systematised by John Searle (1976). In his book *How to do Things with Words,* Austin (1962) argued that sentences could be described as 'true' or 'false' which he contrasted with other utterances the meaning of which could be described in terms of their intended function. A basic distinction was made between *constatives* which could be described in terms of their truth value and *performatives* which could be described in terms of their validity when used under certain conditions. This distinction was later rejected by Austin and he argued that all speech acts should be studied in terms of their illocutionary force. The initial theory was based to a large extent on the special status assigned to 'speech act verbs' which would be indicative of a performative function. Verbs such as *promise* or *bet* were seen to have qualities that would separate them from other kinds of verbs. This initial approach lent itself to corpus analysis and Stubbs (1996) carries out a study of speech act verbs in a corpus. In his research he illustrates that it proves difficult to distinguish the class of verbs conventionally referred to as speech act verbs from other verbs. He shows that the distinction between stative (especially private and reporting verbs) and performative verbs cannot be sustained when they are studied in language-in-use collected in a corpus. Amongst others, he gives the following examples (1996: 216–218):

> "I know he is right."
> "I promise to come."

Neither of these verbs take the *-ing* form in the cases Stubbs analyses, and the simple form of these verbs conveys the speaker's confidence in the truth of the proposition. He concludes that the two cannot be distinguished on either philosophical or linguistic grounds.

From the departure point of distinguishing between truth and falsity in performing particular speech acts outlined above, Austin and Searle move on to a description of the kinds of procedures that are required when performing speech acts and criteria for establishing speaker commitment and authority. The success of an illocution depends on whether a number of *felicity conditions* are met. Searle (1969) formulates four such conditions for speech acts: *propositional, preparatory, sincerity* and *essential.* Of particular relevance to a corpus-based approach to utterance function is the 'essential condition' which, among other aspects, also refers to 'Illocutionary Force Indicating Devices' (hereafter IFID) and states that 'the utterance U contains some IFID which is only properly uttered if all the appropriate conditions apply' (Levinson 1983: 239). Drawing on corpus data, it might be possible to explore the status of particular speech act expressions and verbs as IFIDs.

An example of conditions for requests is given below (Levinson 1983:240):

Propositional content: Future Act A of H
Preparatory: 1. S believes H can do A
                        2. It is not obvious that H would do A without being
                           asked
Sincerity: S wants H to do A
Essential: Counts as an attempt to get H to do A

The status of speech act verbs as IFIDs in explicit performatives is a key feature of the theory developed by Austin and Searle. Yet, there are few other studies which have extended this line of research to investigate whether other possible IFIDs might exist and how these might be best described with the use of real data in context.

A key question is to what extent lexico-grammatical phenomena are part of what constitutes illocutionary force and how they might be grouped in relation to individual speech acts. Searle argues that the 'the meaning of the sentence determines the illocutionary force of its utterances' (1969:143). If we adopt the view that meaning and form are interrelated as illustrated by Sinclair (1996), this would suggest that form and force are also inextricably linked. In a similar vein, Austin suggests that we may be able to identify patterns in linguistic choices which are linked to utterance force and that it may be possible 'to produce a complex criterion, or at least a set of criteria, simple or complex, involving both grammar and vocabulary' (1962:59). Sperber and Wilson (1986:247), quoted in Thibault and van Leeuwen (1996) note in this context:

> What undeniably exists is not a well defined range of syntactic sentence types but a variety of overt linguistic devices – e.g. indicative, imperative or subjunctive mood, rising or falling intonation, inverted or uninverted word order, the presence or absence of Wh-words, or of markers such as 'let's' or 'please' – which can guide the interpretation process in various ways.

Yet, in the absence of suitable corpus data, it is difficult to support such hypotheses. Corpus-based analyses, on the other hand, provide the kind of evidence required to test the loosely formulated hypotheses above. Stubbs (1983b) discusses the fact that surface indicators as a guide to the illocutionary force of individual utterances have largely been ignored in speech act theory. As a consequence, the position which separates syntax and semantics from pragmatics has been strengthened.

2.4.1 Direct and indirect speech acts

In pragmatic theory the notion of 'indirectness' is mainly related to the syntactic form of a sentence in that the illocutionary force is related to the linguistic form of an utterance (declarative, imperative, interrogative = assertion, order/request, question). Both Austin and Searle note, however, that most utterances are indirect, that is, the illocutionary force of many utterances is not reflected in the sentence form. This is mainly due to considerations of politeness and convention when language is used in real contexts.

Grice (1975) notes in this context that a speaker's words often convey more than the literal meaning of the words in the utterance. He argues that the listener interprets the meaning of an utterance with reference to *conversational implicature*. Implicatures are derived via Grice's *co-operative principle* which acts as a benchmark. The co-operative principle is divided into four categories, also called *maxims*: Quantity ('say only as much as is necessary'), Quality ('try to make your contributions one that is true'), Relevance ('be relevant') and Manner ('be brief and avoid ambiguity') (Grice 1975:46). In conversation, however, these maxims are often flouted, and the hearer is forced to derive meaning on the basis of the divergence from a particular maxim.

There have been several criticisms levelled against this theory (see Levinson 1983 for a discussion). Of particular interest for the discussion in this chapter is the lack of consideration of language-in-use in the formulation of the co-operative principle and associated maxims. This applies not only to the relevance and applicability of individual maxims which may be shown to be highly genre and culture specific when studied in the relevant corpora, but also to the wider notion of indirectness which can only be sustained if we accept that hearers derive meaning on the basis of reference to particular maxims. Corpus studies, on the other hand, have shown that many speech acts are conventionalised in nature and may therefore not require reference to the maxims of the co-operative principle.

To address this issue, a distinction between *non-conventional indirect speech acts* and *conventional indirect speech acts* is often made (see, for example, Nattinger & DeCarrico 1992). From a quantitative point of view, corpus analysis mainly lends itself to the study of conventional indirect speech acts, that is, speech acts which habitually display a particular lexico-grammatical construct which is closely associated with a specific function. Non-conventionalised indirect speech acts are those utterances which are potentially multi-functional and therefore require more complicated cognitive procedures for their interpretation. The main focus of this book is therefore on the description of conventionalised speech acts and the speech act expressions associated with them.

One of the most widely discussed conventional indirect speech acts is the indirect request, usually introduced with the speech act expression 'Can you...' (see Aijmer 1996; Searle 1975). While the syntactic structure would suggest a question, corpus evidence shows that this particular speech act expression more often than not introduces a request (see Chapter 3). There are various ways of accounting for the 'indirectness' of an utterance which starts with 'Can you...'. One is to refer to the situational context and inference procedures. The other approach is to study them as conventionalised forms of requests which are habitually introduced with a specific speech act expression. The difference between this type of request and a direct request lies in the extent to which they are explicit. Carter (1998) suggests that there are scales of transparency of fixed expressions. Some can be derived relatively easily from the meaning of their composite parts, such as 'in no uncertain terms' (1998:68), while others are less transparent. Speech act expressions are similar in this respect. However, their level of transparency depends on the degree of conventionalisation, i.e., how often an expression is used as a particular function indicating device.

2.5 Routinisation

There have been various attempts to describe the processes involved in encoding and decoding of conventionalised speech acts. One suggestion is that routinisation, i.e. the recurrent use of a particular speech act expression to realise a particular function, might lead to a form-function composite which is stored as a unit of meaning in its own right. Morgan (1978), for example, points out that an utterance such as *can you pass the salt* is calculable/analysable but not calculated/analysed by the hearer. As such it triggers what he calls a 'short-circuited' implicature (see also Horn 1989) which requires less complex processing procedures on the part of the hearer.

A more radical view has been advanced by Sadock (1974). He deals with the problem of literal meaning of sentences versus intended meaning of utterances with reference to idiomatic expressions. He argues that when there is a mismatch between intended meaning and sentence meaning, the utterance has the same status as an idiomatic expression. Thus, *Can you X* is regarded as an idiomatic expression for *do X* when the intended meaning is that of a request. A similar example is the phrase *why don't you X* which often stands for *do X*, and functions as a suggestion to follow a proposed line of action. These kinds of idioms are different to other, more opaque, types of idioms in that their non-compositionality 'stems from their discoursal uses, since their surface meanings can be readily decoded' (Moon 1997:47).

A number of objections to Sadock's theory were raised at the time (see Levinson 1983 for a discussion), especially in relation to the supposed multi-functionality of such speech act expressions. The argument that a speech act expression such as *Can you* can introduce a request, and hence an indirect speech act, or a question, and thus a direct speech act, led to a general disregard of this theory. It was argued that inference processes would be required to determine whether the expression introduced a direct or indirect speech act (see Levinson 1983). As will be discussed later, this issue only arises when the expression is studied in isolation of the other components of its 'unit of meaning' (Sinclair 1996).

If speech act expressions are treated as units of meaning in the way outlined by Sinclair (1996), it becomes possible to describe their properties in terms of patterns of usage which eliminate a great deal of the functional ambiguity highlighted by Sadock's opponents at the time. Access to spoken corpora has made it possible to study speech act expressions as examples of 'routinised language' (Aijmer 1996) and in terms of their level of 'entrenchment' of meaning as a result of extended usage.

A number of studies have tried to account for the use and processing of speech act expressions and other functional phrases (Fernando 1996; Moon 1994, 1998; Pawley & Syder 1983; Cowie 1988). Nattinger and DeCarrico (1992) discuss examples of indirect speech acts introduced by expressions such as *Can you... X?*. They describe such expressions as existing

> somewhere between the traditional poles of lexicon and syntax, conventionalised form/function composites that occur more frequently and have more idiomatically determined meaning than language that is put together each time.
>
> (Nattinger & DeCarrico 1992:57)

Assuming that the realisation of speech acts relies heavily on some sort of routine formula, they suggest a model of syntactic frames for language teaching purposes which is based on the concept of *syntagmatic simplicity* and *paradigmatic flexibility*. This means that a simple formula on the syntagmatic axis, such as *modal + you + verb phrase* for example, can be seen as a summary of the options on the paradigmatic axis of the phrasal unit.

There are a number of issues with this type of approach. For example, Butler (1988) points out that not all modal items are possible choices on the paradigmatic axis. *Shall*, for example, is not one of the options in the functional frame above. The concept of a functional frame also faces the same criticism that was levelled against Sadock's theory in that it is difficult to distinguish between different functions realised by the same string. Chapter 3 will illustrate how restrictions in the verb phrase might serve as a guide to distinguishing between form/function composites of speech act expressions.

2.6 Functional profiles

The terms *speech act expressions* and *units of meaning* have been used throughout this chapter, and before moving on to a discussion of wider contextual issues it may be useful to further define the relationship between the two. The term *speech act expression* is used here to refer to those phrases and verbs that are closely associated with a particular speech act. Corpus-based analyses of such expressions help establish a prototypical function. In the CANCODE corpus the speech act expression *couldn't you*, for example, is more often used to realise a suggestion than the expression *can't you*, and has therefore acquired a stronger pragmatic function as a suggestion. This kind of pattern becomes part of the 'unit of meaning' of the speech act expression. The notion of the *unit of meaning* is borrowed from Sinclair (1996) and is here used to describe recurring patterns that are part of the speech act expression in the immediate utterance environment, as well as in the discourse and situational environment.

However, given the fact that most existing spoken corpora are still relatively small in size and only provide limited numbers of examples of different speech act expressions in context, more research is needed to make more robust statements about the functional properties of individual expressions. The main objective here is thus to establish *functional profiles* based on the patterns that emerge from quantitative and qualitative analyses. These need to be tested and replicated in order to develop a more robust 'unit of meaning' of a particular speech act expression.

The functional profiles discussed in this book are described according to semantic, as well as pragmatic, properties of the speech act expression. The research draws on Sinclair's (1987) view of the language system as a combination of *open choice principle* and *idiom principle* which is largely consistent with other studies on idiomaticity and formulaticity (Moon 1997; Pawley & Syder 1983; Cowie 1981). This approach is based on the idea that form and meaning are inextricably related. Support for this position comes from a study carried out by Keller (1979). In his work on gambits, or semi-fixed expressions used by speakers to structure the content of a message, he finds that 'a comparison of a large number of gambits from the same category also revealed that at least for some gambits, some of the lexemes making up the expression may be more substitutable than others', and that 'the construction by itself contains some social and semantic information only to be completed and refined by the specific content words to 'fill the slot'(1979:231). Keller refers to the specific construction *Not that..., but....* Here *I disagree with you* could follow the first part, while *I agree with you* stands in semantic opposition to the frame which is used to set the listener at ease and not to condemn his or her opinion altogether. This observation is interesting for the research presented in this volume because it supports a semantic identification of felicity conditions and maintains that there is a relationship between the co-text, the expression and the situation.

The development of functional profiles of speech act expressions as outlined in this book thus tries to shift the focus from inference procedures to form/function composites. The relationship between form and function is here described in terms of recurrent associations in language-in-use. These associations become part of the functional profile of a speech act expression.

2.7 Speech act contexts

Since the interpretation of a particular function of a speech act expression re-lies heavily on the context in which it is used, the description of such contexts becomes a vital part of its functional profile. The role assigned to context in prag-matics compared to corpus linguistics differs quite considerably in that the former relies on context for the interpretation of individual utterances, while the latter is more concerned with making explicit the distribution of lexico-grammatical items and structures across different contexts. A spoken corpus with suitable meta-data about the context in which interactions take place, as well as the relationship between the speakers, would be a useful resource for pragmatic investigations.

So far, mainstream pragmatics has relied mainly on invented contexts to illus-trate the interdependency between speech act function and its place in the wider context of use. Searle (1969:70) gives the example of a wife at a party who an-nounces that 'It's quite late'. He argues that this utterance can be intended as a simple statement of fact, an objection, or a suggestion or request to leave the party. The interpretation of the speech act that Searle describes thus depends both on its place in the ongoing discourse, as well as on situational factors, and speaker rela-tionships. While he uses the example above to illustrate a theoretical point, corpus data enables an analysis of the different functions that the utterance might have by providing the preceding and subsequent discourse, as well as the overall con-text. This approach would, however, require an extended unit of analysis which does not stop at utterance level, but which systematically explores the surrounding discourse.

There are various approaches which have been developed to account for pat-terns at the level of discourse in relation to context. Hymes (1972) proposes a distinction between speech situation, speech events and speech acts. Speech sit-uation refers to activities in a community that have recognisable status, such as 'meals' or 'parties'. In a way, they form a wider category for 'speech events' which are describable by rules of speech, while speech situations are sociological con-structs, associated with the activities in a community rather than with rules for speaking. For example, the 'speech event' of a lecture would be marked by a par-ticular structural organisation, as well as a specific distribution of speaker roles. Speech acts, on the other hand, occur within speech events and speech situations and are to some extent governed by them. According to Hymes (1972), the speech act encodes social norms in linguistic form. The interpretation of speech acts thus leads to an analysis of the sequential organisation in discourse, as well as to an analysis of the social roles of the speakers in the particular context they are engaged in at the time.

The types of inference procedures proposed by Leech (1983) and Brown and Levinson (1987) rely predominantly on the (shared) internal knowledge of the speaker and hearer, but there is little discussion of knowledge of explicit contextual categories and conventions. Other researchers have tried to outline the kind of knowledge about the constraints that a particular situation puts on possible contributions in an interaction. Speakers and hearers refer to a 'frame' or a 'schema' around which they orient themselves when they speak (Aijmer 1996; Cook 1994; Brown & Yule 1983; Coulmas 1979). Aijmer (1996:27) argues that the 'frame should be regarded as a hypothesis about speakers' stereotypic knowledge of a situation and how this knowledge is organised in the long-term memory.' A frame includes criteria such as the identity of the participants, the setting and the reason for the interaction (see Coulmas 1979). As situations recur, certain ways to perform speech acts recur and become conventionalised, such as greetings and good-byes at a party.

One area that has focused on establishing 'categories' that account for the relationship between language and situation is 'genre theory' (Mitchell 1957; Hasan 1985, 1999; Ventola 1987; Hammond & Derewianka 2001). Many accounts within genre theory are based on the assumption that speech events are describable in terms of 'stages' that are either optional or compulsory in the completion of the event. While this kind of categorisation aids the broad description of genres, a closer inspection of spoken discourse-in-use highlights the dynamic character of genre orientation which in turn makes it difficult to apply schemata to whole conversations.

Aijmer (1996:27) argues that 'Exactly what situational factors are needed in a frame depends not only on what speech act is studied, but also on one's theory of what the factors of the communication situation are.' While it is useful to outline various factors that are intuitively important for relating the speech act expression to a particular context, such lists of criteria could potentially be lengthy and difficult to evaluate in an empirical manner. A more promising approach is to analyse a large number of instances of a particular speech act expression in its discourse context and list emergent patterns that may be related to the context of the situation. There are certain variables that can be controlled in such an approach, including, for example, the relationship between the speaker and the setting, as well as the type of interaction, i.e., whether it is a monologue or a dialogue, etc. The next section looks in more detail at the relationship between corpus design categories, which carry contextual information, and their applicability to the study of linguistic choices which are contextually motivated.

2.8 Spoken corpus design and contextual information: An example

The contextual dependencies of linguistic choices are well documented and theorised (Hasan 1999; Swales 2004). Research in the area of corpus linguistics over the past two decades has generated ample evidence for the linguistic variation between different context types (Biber 1988; Reppen et al. 2002). Variation in linguistic choice is not only associated with distinctly different contexts, such as spoken and written discourse, but has also been linked to more subtle differences in context, such as exist in conversations between friends compared to conversations between family members (McCarthy 1998).

In order to be able to establish the link between linguistic variation and different contexts, it is important to have access to suitably categorised spoken corpora which reflect the kinds of contexts which are commonly recognised and which are external to the language itself. In the following section, an example of contextual categorisation of a spoken corpus is introduced to highlight possible issues of corpus design and resulting research opportunities and limitations. The corpus that is used here as an example is the Cambridge and Nottingham Corpus of Discourse in English (CANCODE) (see also McCarthy 1998 for an extensive discussion of the CANCODE corpus project). Many other spoken corpora exist, each following their own categorisation scheme. At the same time, many of the 'second generation mega-corpora' (Kennedy 1998: 45) include spoken components. The coverage in terms of genre and demographic spread tends to be broader in these corpora than in the early, first generation ones. However, the type of spoken data contained in such corpora are still a major issue in the debate on representativeness of corpora. The COBUILD project, for example, includes radio-broadcasting, as well as university archives of interviews and lectures, whilst the 10 million word spoken part of the British National Corpus includes data collected in formal situations, such as political forums and business events, and also conversations of people going about their day-to-day business. The spoken demographic (or conversational) component of the BNC was designed to be balanced in terms of sociolinguistic variables, rather than discourse contexts, and represents a random sample in terms of location (see Aston & Burnard 1998). The variation in the types of contexts recorded as part of different spoken corpora, as well as in the parameters used for collecting data, makes it difficult to accumulate a large enough sample of spoken data that follows the same design principles. As a result, research based on spoken corpora is often limited in terms of the number of examples of a particular linguistic feature in the corpus, especially once contextual filters have been applied.

However, there have been a number of attempts to assemble spoken corpora which follow the same design, not only to grow the overall resource in a consistent manner, but also to allow comparisons between different varieties. One of the corpora that has been designed to follow the same categorisation scheme as CANCODE is the Limerick Corpus of Irish English (LCIE) (see Farr et al. 2004 for a description). The parallel design of the two resources affords a comparison of different varieties of English across the same contexts.

To illustrate a possible contextual categorisation scheme and associated issues, the CANCODE corpus will be considered in more detail. CANCODE was developed at the University of Nottingham, UK, mainly between 1994 and 2001, and was funded by Cambridge University Press, with whom sole copyright resides. The conversations in the corpus were recorded in a wide variety of mostly informal settings across the UK and Ireland, then transcribed and stored in computer-readable form.

In spite of the trend to develop ever larger multi-million word corpora, in the case of CANCODE the main aim has been to construct a corpus which can allow both quantitative and qualitative investigation. With its overall size of 5 million words, it allows for quantitative analysis of high frequency items, while at the same time providing carefully transcribed records of conversations for the use of discourse analysts.

The conversations in the corpus were collected with reference to a range of different speech genres with an emphasis on 'casual conversation'. A classification scheme was developed to make corpus internal comparisons, especially with regard to the effect of speaker relationships on linguistic choices. In CANCODE, traditional divisions between formal and informal, structured versus unstructured and monologue versus dialogue, have been used as general guiding principles for data collection. The framework used for the CANCODE corpus includes two axes for classification, the *context-type* and *interaction type*.

2.8.1 Context-types

This axis of categorization reflects the relationship that holds between the participants in the dyadic and multi-party conversations in the corpus. The types of relationship fall into five broad categories which were identified at the outset: *intimate, socio-cultural, professional, transactional* and *pedagogic*. These categories were found to be largely exclusive while being comprehensive at the same time. In multi-party conversations where different relationships hold between different speakers, it turned out that speakers would converge towards one type of relationship category. Thus, two friends would adopt a 'professional' attitude when in the company of colleagues. Often this convergence was related to the particular purpose of the encounter in that colleagues who were also friends would adopt a 'socio-cultural' attitude when with other friends at a party. However, an interaction between a doctor who is making a house visit and family members in the house would still be classified as *transactional,* as the purpose of the conversation is still related to this category.

In the *intimate* category the distance between the speakers is at a minimum and is often related to co-habitation. Only conversations between partners or close family qualify for this category in which participants are most 'off-guard'. The *socio-cultural* category implies the voluntary interaction between speakers who seek each other's company for the sake of the interaction itself. The relationship between the speakers is usually marked by friendship and is thus not as close as that between speakers in the *intimate* category. The *professional* category was used to refer to the relationship that holds between people who are interacting as part of their regular daily work. As such, this category only applies to interactions where all speakers are part of the professional context. The *transactional* category includes interactions in which the speakers do not know one another, and is often found in 'goods-and-services' encounters where the exchange of goods is one of the main aims of the interaction (Ventola 1987). The *pedagogic* category includes any interaction in which the relationship between the speakers is defined by the pedagogic context, such as is the case in tutorials, seminars and lectures. As the emphasis here is on the speaker relationship rather than the setting, conversations between lecturers, as well as academic staff meetings were classified as *professional* rather than *pedagogic.* At the same time, training sessions in companies were classified as *pedagogic* rather than *professional.*

Corpus searches can be sorted by relationship category so that the concordance output directly displays the contextual origin of individual uses of particular words or phrases, as is illustrated in the sample of 30 concordance lines of *Why not* below:

socio-cultural	\<S03\> Well	**why not?**	
professional	\<S03\>	**Why not?**	
professional	\<S01\>	**Why not?**	
socio-cultural		**Why not?**	
socio-cultural	\<S02\>	**Why not?**	
intimate	\<S01\>	**Why not?**	
transactional	\<S03\>	**Why not?**	
intimate	\<S01\>	**Why not?**	
pedagogic	\<S01\>	**Why not?**	
socio-cultural	you know	**why not**	sort of make it a
professional		**Why not**	just make gradual
pedagogic	teals one and	**why not**	sing his salmon w
intimate		**Why not?**	
intimate		**Why not?**	
socio-cultural		**Why not?**	
intimate	I don't see	**why not.**	

intimate				<S01>	**Why not?**	
intimate				<S01>	**Why not?**	
socio-cultural			<S01> I said	"**Why not?**"		
intimate				<S02>	**Why not?**	
intimate			said "Well	**why not?**"		
intimate				<S01>	**Why not?**	
professional			all that is	**why not**	use erm </$=>.	
socio-cultural			</$E> And	**why not.**		
socio-cultural			I don't see	**why not**		
intimate			I don't see	**why not**		
pedagogic				**Why not**	pick ones from ea	
socio-cultural			<$?F>	**Why not**	ask <$G?>.	
socio-cultural		police is well		**why not**	put some sort of	
professional		to you Well		**why not**	just put the loan	

The contextual classification scheme used for the CANCODE corpus is based on the degree of *distance* between speakers. External criteria have been applied in the design which allow for a relatively unbiased study of linguistic patterns according to external contexts. Yet, the categories are largely intuitive and further sociological research is needed to test the validity of the categories themselves. It is also not clear whether the relationship between the speakers is a valid organising principle for context. It could be argued that the 'goal' of the interaction is more important than the relationship that holds between the speakers. The categorisation scheme that was designed for CANCODE tried to take account of different goal-types although the highly dynamic nature of goals in discourse made it difficult to apply such a categorisation to complete texts. The goal-types in the corpus were explicitly related to *interaction-types*.

2.8.2 Interaction-types

When deciding on the interaction-type axis in the CANCODE corpus, the traditional classification of *dialogue* versus *monologue* adopted by many previous corpus designers (see Kennedy 1998: 72) was considered too narrow. All of the texts in CANCODE are to some extent dialogic, yet certain features of non-collaborative discourse can be identified. A further distinction within the collaborative texts was made between *collaborative idea* and *collaborative task*. *Collaborative task* is akin to what Hasan (1999: 276) calls *material action*. Typical situations in which we would expect collaborative task interactions are service encounters which involve the exchange of a physical object. Similarly, any interaction in which language is ancillary or complementary, with reference to a physical entity or event, would fall under this category. Language is usually less explicit in collaborative task situations than in interactions where an idea is collaboratively developed. The category of collaborative idea is the largest category in the CANCODE corpus and applies to all conversations in which participants engage in a collaborative construction of discourse. Non-collaborative texts are those in which speakers give explanations and information or relate events and tell stories. At a discourse level, such accounts usually remain uninterrupted apart from the occasional backchannel from other speakers. Since these conversations are marked by the unidirectional transfer of information from one speaker to other interactants, this type has been termed *information provision*.

McCarthy (1998) refers to the interaction types in the classification model as *goal-types*, which are associated more closely with genre categories rather than with text structure. However, the interaction types are closely related to text-types in that the overall goal of information provision will be mirrored in the unidirectional text structure.

While the categorisation of speaker relationship is relatively straightforward as its components are easily recognised by members of a particular speech community, the categorisation of goal-types is more difficult to apply. The reason for this is related to the problem of embedding of text-types. Thus, while a number of texts such as lectures, for example, can easily be identified as belonging to the interaction type *information provision*, other interactions, especially casual conversation, but also service encounters and interviews, display a high degree of switching of interaction types. This phenomenon has been highlighted in previous studies (Eggins & Slade 1997; Hasan 1999; Ventola 1987) and causes particular problems when the interaction type is used as a design category. In many texts, the category *information provision*, which may apply to someone telling a story, is interrupted by a more 'open' floor where other participants interrupt and contribute to the conversation, thus changing it to a more collaborative interaction. A similar tendency has been discussed by Eggins and Slade (1997:231). They differentiate between *chat* and *chunk* which both regularly occur in casual conversation and other highly interactive genres. While *chat* is marked by its fast change of turns and irregularity with respect to topic and coherence, a *chunk* segment is describable in generic terms. Defining smaller units within a conversation in terms of their interaction type is beyond the scope of most spoken corpus projects, and since there is little understanding about the nature of genre embedding it may be unfeasible altogether.

Similar difficulties arise when we compare *collaborative idea* with *collaborative task*. *Collaborative task* sequences are regularly embedded in the *collaborative idea* interaction-type, especially when a task accompanies verbal action, for example when people are chatting while preparing a meal. Speakers will temporarily refer to a physical object and then 'switch back' to the ongoing conversation. On the other hand, *collaborative task* conversations are often accompanied by long stretches of *collaborative idea* and 'information provision'. The following extract illustrates this

Line		
1	<S04>	That's your favourite name isn't it+
2	<S03>	<$G?>
3	<S04>	+Alison.
4	<S06>	<$G?>
5	<S01>	Alison. Is it? I've never <$G4>.
6	<S06>	Well they call <$H> her </$H> Alison Sarah.
7	<S03>	<$G?>
8	<S04>	I thought it was going to be Alison Amy <$H> one time </$H>.
9	<S01>	No. <$E> laughs </$E>
10	<S02>	No. Amelia is er brilliant.
11	<S01>	Evy+
12	<S03>	Never missed in six years <$H> news </$H>.
13	<S05>	<$=> How do you </$=>
14	<S01>	+like me.
15	<S05>	You have to bounce it.
16	<S01>	And then Alison Sarah.
17	<S03>	That's the secret.
18	<$?F>	<$G?>
19	<S01>	Bounced away.
20	<S03>	Take it off and see if you can do it again properly.
21	<S05>	Okay.
22	<S03>	And I bet you can't.
23	<S04>	Why don't you press+ <S02> Come on.
24	<S03>	Right.
25	<S04>	+them together and see+
26	<S03>	Come on my dear.
27	<S04>	+if they they go <$G3>.
28	<S05>	<$G2> I'll try.
29	<S04>	You need a secretary.
30	<S05>	Shall I bounce it Pete?
31	<S07>	Good grief.
32	<$?F>	<$G?>
33	<S03>	No. Only as far as it goes in. It doesn't matter what it bounces off.
34	<S01>	<$G2>
35	<S03>	A bit straightforward that was.
36	<S04>	What looks like the possibility+
37	<S05>	All right. Then I'll do a special one.
38	<S04>	+throw out a possibility and+
39	<S03>	Yeah.
40	<S04>	+throw it onto this diary here. <$=> And see if it </$=>
41	<S03>	<$=> Are we talking </$=> Which month are we talking about?
42	<S02>	Ah no.
43	<S05>	<$G?> <$E> briefly unintelligible </$E>
44	<S05>	Well in February Mum <$=> we're going </$=> we might be going down down
45		to the Smith's mightn't we.

46	<S07>	You'll be lucky.
47	<S02>	Oh yeah. <$G?>
48	<S01>	<$=> I wish we were </$=>
49	<S03>	<$=> Are we talk </$=> Bryan. Are we talking about February or March?
50	<$?F>	<$E> laughs </$E>
51	<S07>	March I think <$=> would be a better </$=>+

point. The text has been classified as 'collaborative task' in the corpus and falls into the *socio-cultural* category.

In this multi-party conversation the participants are first discussing names for children (lines 1–12, 14, 16–18). This is interrupted by a short sequence of collaborative task in which one of the participants is taking a photo (lines 13, 15, 19–35, 37). When the task is completed, the speakers resume a conversation which concerns a date on which they will next meet (lines 36, 38+). While the sequence in the middle of the extract can be identified as collaborative task, there seems to be a difference between the first part of this extract and the third part in that the goal of the two is different. McCarthy (1998) therefore distinguishes between various sub-goals in one goal type, such as *decision making* or *problem solving*. These sub-goal-types seem to be a more appropriate classification category, however, they need to be established through a close analysis of individual discourse stretches and are unsuitable for broader corpus design purposes.

As far as the analysis of speech act expressions in the CANCODE corpus is concerned, the discussion above shows that while the corpus lends itself to a comparison of the distribution of such expressions across different speaker relationship categories, an analysis of distribution across interaction-types is problematic. Individual goal-sub-types have to be established based on the immediate discourse environment in which speech act expressions occur. However, since such goal-sub-types are dynamic in nature, they cannot be based on the interaction-type classification.

2.8.3 Further issues in spoken corpus design

In addition to the contextual categorisation issues outlined above, spoken corpus design and compilation faces a range of further issues which deserve further discussion. Analyses and emerging results based on spoken corpus data need to be interpreted in the light of the decisions made at the design stage, and judged against the backdrop of the overall compilation and representation strategy applied to the data.

One of the key issues in corpus design is the issue of representativeness, whether this refers to language as a whole as used by a particular group of speakers, or to the contextual categories established by corpus designers. In terms of coverage of different contexts, one of the initial aims in the design process of CANCODE was to collect an equal number of words in each of the contextual categories identified at the outset. This was to ensure representativeness and to create a base for comparison between the different categories. However, it soon emerged that certain situations occur less often than others. Unidirectional discourse in intimate encounters, for example, is very rare, and the low word count in this category is thus not a reflection of the representativeness of the data in the corpus, but more indicative of the occurrence of this type of interaction in general. Furthermore, with a focus on 'casual conversation', a low proportion of 'information provision' discourse, and a high word count in the *socio-cultural* context-type, seemed to provide a better representation of the kind of every-day interaction that the corpus set out to cover. The initial aim of collecting equal numbers of words in each category was therefore abandoned and the final corpus ended up being varied with regard to the frequency counts in the different categories. Comparisons across the different contexts therefore have to be made in terms of relative frequencies.

A wider concern related to the notion of representativeness when it comes to broader descriptions of language, is that a corpus-based approach might skew the results in a way that is a direct reflection of the selections of texts in the corpus. Furthermore, there are issues related to the fact that corpora are records of production rather than reception and might therefore not adequately represent the language experience of speakers of a language. Cook (1998) highlights that the notion of *reception* is often neglected in corpus construction or analysis: 'They contain information about production but not about reception. They say nothing about how many people have read or heard a text or utterance, or how many times' (Cook 1998: 58).

The question of whether any one corpus can ever adequately represent the language commonly used in a particular situation, or by a particular group of speakers, needs further exploration and discussion. In the meantime, it is important that the categorisation schemata applied for the purpose of corpus design are outlined explicitly when results are reported. This process necessitates the collection of meta-data and the careful cataloguing of such data as part of the corpus-design process.

Here it is important to distinguish between *contextual information* and *textual information*, although the two are not always easily distinguished in spoken discourse. *Contextual information* is normally added in a separate database, or in the form of a 'header' to individual files. For any spoken corpus this might include a variety of different kinds of information, including the age and sex of the speakers, where they live, their educational background, etc. Once this kind of information is recorded, the corpus can be used as a resource for comparisons across those variables.

In terms of *textual information*, the spoken corpus developer has to decide on appropriate transcription conventions for the recorded conversations, considering a range of cost/benefit issues in relation to the main research aim (see Thompson 2005). Since transcription costs tend to account for the best part of the budget in spoken corpus projects, simple orthographic transcription is often regarded as sufficient for lexicography purposes. However, this type of transcription does not account for many aspects of the original speech event that may have been of importance to the speakers and hearers at the time, and that may well play a part in the retrospective interpretation of an utterance. Both prosodic information and body language of participants, as well as the physical setting, may influence the conversation at the time (Cook 1990; McCarthy 2000). Since the context of the situation could potentially be infinite, so could be the transcription features recorded in the text (Cook 1990).

The majority of current spoken corpora are not presented in a multi-modal way, and do not allow the researcher access to sound or video recordings of the original data. As a result, it can be difficult to assign a particular pragmatic function to an utterance in cases where intonation is the determining factor for the interpretation. More recent projects which develop and explore multi-modal corpora have started to establish the relationship between patterns at the textual, prosodic and gestural level, and it will be interesting to see whether such elements might be combined to form part of a multi-modal unit of meaning.

The process of transcription requires a substantial amount of analytical decision making. It is therefore important to recognise that a transcript is always an analysed text to a certain degree. Yet, this kind of analysis is necessary in order to find a representational format for the recorded interactions. Further analytical data can be added by researchers at a later stage, and there are a number of projects which have been concerned with annotating corpus resources with functional information (see Stockley 2006 and Weisser 2003 on the use of automatic speech act annotation tools), as well as with information about speech and thought presentation (see Semino & Short 2004).

In deciding on categories that are implicated in the design of a spoken corpus, certain assumptions are made about the relevance of such factors as 'speaker relationship', 'age', 'sex' etc. for the interpretation of discourse. This is, of course, not an approach which is unique to corpus design but one that can be found in many different areas of language study. This includes the area of pragmatics where theories of politeness regularly draw on contextual categories related to the formality of the situation and speaker relationship. Yet, we cannot be sure how relevant these aspects are to the participants at the time of the interaction itself. Neither is it always reliable to elicit such information after the interaction has taken place as participants might not themselves be able to recollect their own interpretations at a later stage. Contextual categories applied to corpus data therefore have to be regarded as provisional until enough evidence can be found to indicate a strong relationship between individual categories and language use.

However, close analysis of emerging patterns within texts appear to provide a better basis for understanding interpretative processes than accounts that are based on the analyst's intuition alone.

2.9 Summary

This chapter has illustrated ways in which a corpus-based approach to the analysis of language functions challenges traditional paradigms, especially in the area of pragmatics. These include the notion of *indirect speech acts* and the *explicit performative*. It has been argued that a description of speech act expressions in terms of their unit of meaning which includes patterns of collocation, colligation, and discoursal placement, makes the distinction between pragmatic and semantic meaning unnecessary. Chapters 3, 4 and 5 outline a general approach to support such a description.

This chapter has also considered in more detail the notion of context in relation to corpus design and analysis. Functional analyses have to be carried out with reference to discourse co-text, as well as to the wider context in which individual speech act expressions occur. However, definitions of context vary as do contextual design criteria for different corpora. It is therefore important to make such criteria explicit at the outset of any analysis, and to discuss any analytical results in the light of the initial corpus design.

The next chapter looks at possible frameworks for analysing speech act expressions in a spoken corpus, both from a concordance perspective and from a discourse perspective.

CHAPTER 3

Pragmatic functions, speech act expressions and corpus evidence

3.0 Introduction

Following on from the discussion of the use of corpora in the study of pragmatic functions in chapters 1 and 2, this chapter looks at a particular speech act, that of making suggestions, to illustrate how a close analysis of corpus data can inform pragmatic theories and methodologies. The chapter begins with a description of *suggestions* as a speech act and considers the interface between data and theory, drawing on examples from a spoken corpus. A sample analysis of a particular set of speech act expressions associated with the speech act of *making suggestions* follows the initial outline of theoretical and practical issues.

3.1 Lexico-grammar and speech acts

In order to be able to use the construct of speech act function as an organising principle for empirical investigation, the function itself needs to be defined at the outset. Within the area of pragmatics, there are various frameworks for categorising different speech act functions. However, these do not always correspond to the semantics of the speech act verbs which describe the categories, nor to the conventionalised ways of expressing particular functions. The former thus has to be seen as a meta-category, while the close analysis of speech act verbs, as well as speech act expressions, should enable the development of individual functional profiles of such verbs and expressions.

Austin (1962) highlights the fact that there are a number of verbs in the English language that describe the speech acts which we regularly perform in everyday interaction, such as *order, command, ask,* etc. However, while there is a large number of such verbs, they do not all mark different illocutionary points (see Searle 1976). Yet, verbs that do mark the same illocutionary point, might have different functional profiles when analysed in a corpus. Tsui (1994), for example, argues that the verbs *suggest* and *advise* are, in fact, different verbs which describe the same act. Tsui's argument is based on two examples taken from a corpus in which the two verbs appear to be interchangeable. However, a study of a larger sample of the two verbs in a corpus is necessary to establish their functional profiles. This will allow an assessment of whether or not they realise the same illocutionary point.

The same applies to more indirect conventionalised ways of performing speech acts, such as those introduced by the speech act expressions *how about, what about, why not, let's* and *can't you*. While these do not constitute speech act categories as such, they should be treated in the same way as performative verbs when it comes to the description of their illocutionary force or functional profile in a corpus. Previous research of such speech act expressions has explored their pragmatic properties. One of the distinctions that has been made in the discussion of different functions is between expressions that, at a semantic level, include the speaker, such as *why don't we* and *let's*, and those that only include the hearer, such as *why don't you* or *maybe you should* (Tsui 1994). The rationale for making such a distinction lies in the 'rate of the imposition' (Brown & Levinson 1987) which is higher when the 'burden' of the suggestion is on the hearer rather than on both the hearer and the speaker. However, there are problems in using this approach without consulting a corpus. A corpus might show, for example, that an inclusive expression such as *let's* + *verb* does not always, or even habitually, realise an inclusive suggestion, especially since it may have lost some of the meaning of its constituent parts due to extended usage.

The discussion in this chapter aims to illustrate that extended usage can override the semantics of the individual composite parts of such a string, which comes to acquire a meaning and function in its own right. Since pragmatic theories as well as related theories of politeness are based to some extent on the semantics of utterances, corpus-based approaches which analyse speech acts as extended units of meaning are likely to generate the kind of results which call for a different interpretation to those traditionally found in the literature on speech acts.

3.2 Defining speech acts: The example of suggestions

In order to illustrate the difficulty in using a corpus-based approach to analyse language functions, it is important to explore the implications of a possible reconciliation of positions. As already discussed, the pragmatic approach starts from a functional perspective, while the corpus approach starts from a lexico-grammatical perspective. If we study a particular set of functions in a corpus and adopt a definition of such functions which has been developed without reference to corpus data, we subscribe to a set of assumptions that might not be relevant to the functional profiles we aim to establish. Yet, in order to arrive at better descriptions of language functions, we need to start with a functional categorisation as an organising principle. This section considers in more detail the way in which individual functions might be described and defined in abstract terms. It also considers the effect of such descriptions when they are imposed as an organising principle in the identification of particular functions in a corpus. The example of making suggestions has been chosen to illustrate this process.

Speech act functions have been defined in different ways and previous research includes reference to grammatical and lexico-grammatical descriptions (Halliday 1985; Sinclair & Coulthard 1975; Green 1972), as well as philosophical parameters (see Levinson 1983 for an overview). As outlined in the previous chapter, Searle's (1976) model, for example, is based entirely on felicity conditions. Suggestions come closest to Searle's (1969) category of *Advisement* – a subcategory of directives, in which the speaker assigns some benefit to the hearer (1969:67). Searle's categorisation is based on the notion of *speaker goal* in the conversation, which is first and foremost to get the hearer to recognise the speaker's intention. One of the main problems with the inclusion of *speaker goals* as a component of the descriptive apparatus is that such goals are not accessible to the analyst. Instead, they have to rely on the actual text for interpretation. However, there are further issues with classification schemes such as the one suggested by Searle as illustrated in the following extract.

Line		
1	\<S02\>	\<$O42\> **Let's be quite honest** \</$O42\> you've got to have a pretty warped
2		sense of humour to nick three bags of crap and an essay.
3	\<S01\>	Well some people do though don't they.
4	\<S03\>	Well if they nick the car \<$O43\> \<$G?\> \</$O43\>
5	\<S04\>	\<$O43\> They'll probably \</$O43\> leave your \<$G?\>
6	\<S01\>	\<$O43\> \<$G?\> **I would suggest** \</$O43\> that we take your bag inside then
7		\<$O44\> you'll feel happier \</$O44\>.
8	\<S02\>	\<$O44\> But that's what I said. \</$O44\>

In this extract there are two instances of verbs which have been associated with making suggestions: *let's* (line 1) and *suggest* (line 6). Both suggestions include the speaker, at least at a semantic level, in the proposed line of action. This presents the first problem with Searle's classification. If the speaker commits himself or herself to an action, then these utterances should count as *commissives*. However, since they also include the hearer, they should be *directives*. Suggestions are particularly problematic in this context and the overall impasse created by their functionally hybrid character has been widely recognised. Halliday (1985) highlights that '[o]ffers and commands, and also suggestions which are simply the combination of the two (offer: 'I'll do it', command 'you do it', suggestion 'let's do it'), can be projected paratactically in the same way as propositions' (1985:235). He argues further that 'the most fundamental types of speech role, which lie behind all the more specific types that we may eventually be able to recognise, are just two: (i) giving, and (ii) demanding' (1985:68). His position is similar to that of Tsui (1994) in that he links lexico-grammar to speech act function, i.e. *let's do it* is classed as a suggestion. This adds to the confusion of classifying relatively fixed speech act expressions such as *let's be honest* outlined above. In Halliday's framework a speech act is an 'interact' and as such requires a specific response in order to be recognised as carrying a particular function. The speech role of giving would thus presuppose the act of receiving. By including reference to the uptake of speech roles, Halliday's framework cannot easily account for relatively fixed speech act expressions such as *let's be honest* for example in which the nature of the 'interact' is less clear.

Both suggestions in the extract above are difficult to classify, albeit for different reasons. The utterance *let's be honest* uses a speaker inclusive contraction and uses an imperative form. Looking at a concordance output of *let's* in the CANCODE corpus, it becomes clear that the main function of this expression is a structuring one, rather than a speech act function. It is used as part of the meta-discourse that participants engage in, and structuring this discourse is its main purpose. The same applies to other multi-word expressions introduced with *let's*, such as *let's assume* and *let's think*, which, although more semantically explicit, still remain difficult to classify in terms of traditional speech act classification models.

The second suggestion in the extract above also poses difficulties for traditional classification models. The speaker inclusion suggests a *commissive* whilst the hearer inclusion and hearer benefit would imply an *advisement*. The analyst cannot know who will, in the end, carry the bags inside, and neither does this seem to be important for the participants in this conversation. The fact that many suggestions in real conversations are difficult to classify in terms of their status as *directives* or *commissives* has been linked to their interpersonal value in interaction. DeCapua and Huber (1995:124) point out that in equal status encounters, advice giving 'may be used as a rapport-building mechanism.' Speakers may not, in the first instance, seek to get the hearer to do something or to solve a particular problem, but rather to 'ascertain shared values and intimacy'(ibid). As a result, agency becomes less important as a goal, and the focus shifts towards convergence between the speakers.

An approach which the semantics of an utterance tries to map onto the kinds of functional categories established within speech act theory thus results in a situation where suggestions are positioned awkwardly between *commissives* and *directives* or *offers* and *commands*. The analysis of corpus data, on the other hand, appears to indicate that these categories only play a minor role in the description of the functions associated with the lexico-grammatical constructs used to make suggestions.

3.3 Speech act classification and discourse analysis

Using a discourse perspective in the analysis of speech acts is an important step towards solving some of the problems of the initial speech act classification models which were based entirely on individual utterances. As highlighted above, Halliday incorporates a discourse level analysis into his classification scheme. Similarly, Sinclair & Coulthard (1975) integrate discourse factors, as well as some lexico-grammatical features, into their framework and define acts by their interactive function. They differentiate between *meta-discursive, interactive* and *turn-taking acts* in their model which is mainly based on classroom data. Many adaptations have since emerged which apply the model to conversational and other types of data (see for example Tsui 1994; Burton 1981).

Tsui (1994) differentiates between three primary classes of acts based on the three moves of an exchange as defined by Sinclair and Coulthard (1975): *initiating acts, responding acts* and *follow-up acts*. Her classification criteria for the different speech act classes are based on intended speaker response, which makes her framework more tangible than Searle's model. Her initiating acts are linked to the following interactive functions:

	Discourse Function
Elicitations	elicit an obligatory verbal response or its non-verbal surrogate
Requestives	solicit non-verbal action with the option to carry out this action
Directives	solicit non-verbal action with no option of whether or not the addressee will carry out the solicited action
Informatives	provide information and to report events and states of affairs, recount personal experience, etc.

Tsui argues that

> requestives subsume utterances which have been referred to in the speech act literature, as requests, invite, ask for permission, and offer. They do not subsume those which have been referred to as order, command, and instruct. The latter are subsumed under a different subclass: directives (1994:91).

According to Tsui's classification, *suggestions* are therefore a subcategory of *directives*. She distinguishes between *mandatives*, which direct the addressee to perform an action for the benefit of the speaker, and *advisives*, which direct the addressee to perform an action for his/her own benefit.

While Tsui's model takes discourse level structures into account, it cannot easily accommodate suggestions such as those in the extract above either. Utterances such as *I would suggest that we take your bag inside* are neither *mandatives* nor *advisives*. She therefore creates a further category, which are a sub-class of requestives, and which she calls *proposals*. A *proposal* or *suggestion*, according to Tsui, 'prospect both speaker action and addressee action and is typically realised by Can/Could/Shall we do X?'(Tsui 1994:100). It is beneficial to both speaker (S) and addressee (A).

Requestives:

	Speaker action	Addressee action	S+A action
Speaker benefit	Request for permission	Request for action	
Addressee benefit	Offer	invitation	
S+A benefit			proposal

Tsui (1994:104)

The use of cost/benefit scales is appealing but creates its own problems when we consider actual data. This will be further discussed in the next section.

3.3.1 Problems with cost benefit scales

Tsui's 'typical' realisations for proposals are based on the inclusive pronoun *we*, which, as she argues, prospects both speaker and hearer action. However, the suggestion *I would suggest that we take your bag inside then you'll feel happier* is not only de-focalised in terms of commitment, but is also for the benefit of the addressee, a category missing in Tsui's classification. The benefit of a particular action is not always easy to assign to individual participants in conversation as the following examples from the CANCODE corpus illustrate:

Line	
1	<S01> That was in <$E> place name <\$E> wasn't it. **Shall we say everyone's name so**
2	**that we know who everyone is on the tape.**
3	<S04> <$E> spells name <\$E>
4	<S01> MX and I'm FX the interviewer. Please.
5	<S03> I'm FX
6	<S02> And I'm MX. MX.
7	<S01> So everyone knows.

Here, it is difficult to assign speaker or hearer benefit. Rather, the suggestion is aimed to support the successful completion of a specific task in this context. Contextual dependencies are thus important to take into account when we assess cost and benefit. In existing frameworks these two polar categories are usually conceived of in isolation and detached from any context and speaker relationship. In the following extract, two speakers are involved in a business meeting and speaker 2 makes a suggestion to address a problem outlined by speaker 1.

Line		
1	\<S01\>	Erm basically we've come to something of an impasse because the costs of doing
2		a CD Rom were incredibly high to record all those words and also the technology
3		\<$=\> is still erm er \<\\$=\>it's still going to be very difficult to fit as much onto a
4		CD as we want to. Erm so we decided not to go ahead with that on our own but
5		the option that's still open to us is er we're going to look for a software house erm
6		i= to see if we can share the costs of development with somebody who would like
7		to have the data the sound files for research that they're doing. So we think that
8		might be a possible area to go into. So if we can pull off that sort of thing we may
9		still go ahead with a CD Rom but erm in the near future erm it won't be going
10		ahead.
11	\<S02\>	\<$=\> Er why not er \<\\$=\> **Why not do an ordinary CD audio rather than CD**
12		**Rom?** \<$G3\>
13	\<S01\>	Well what would you do with it? You can't really sit there and listen to one \<$O13\>
14		word after another \<\\$O13\>.

Again, the 'cost' of this suggestion is difficult to assess and the benefit relates to the particular task at hand, rather than the speaker or the hearer. The professional context in which the two speakers interact determines the goal-directed nature of the conversation and changes the focus of the cost/benefit scale which has traditionally been related directly to the speaker and hearer. The complexity of cost and benefit as constructs, which are dynamic and highly context dependent, makes them difficult to apply to real data.

The extract also highlights a further issue which arises when cost/benefit scales are linked to the semantics of an utterance. Speech act expressions which do not include a personal pronoun, such as *how about* and *why not*, are difficult to classify in a framework such as the one proposed by Tsui (1994). It is not clear whether they should count as *proposals*, *advisives* or *mandatives*. Using the response types to these utterances as a guide for interpretation is not always helpful either, as many suggestions are followed by a minimal response by the hearer. This makes it difficult to establish the function of the preceding utterance.

3.4 Speech acts as strategies?

In order to get around the problem created by the mismatch between semantic categories and speech act function, it could be argued that speech act expressions are sometimes used literally and other times used as a strategy (see Brown & Levinson 1987; Kasper 1990). Thus, if, at the lexico-grammatical level, the speaker implies 'speaker inclusiveness', by using pronouns such as *we* or the contracted form *let's* (let us), whilst he or she actually does not intend any commitment, then the utterance must be seen as a politeness strategy. If, on the other hand, the speaker intends commitment, then the utterance has to be taken literally. In the absence of real data-in-use, it is understandable how such a position can develop. However, as the two extracts above have shown it may not be necessary to distinguish between literal and pragmatic meaning. The surrounding discourse can provide clues as to the way in which an utterance was intended. The strategic value of indirectness in terms of signalling politeness, for example, thus requires further exploration (see also Blum-Kulka 1987).

The example of *let's* discussed above shows that the exploration of corpus data suggests that traditional criteria for speech act classification may be less relevant, as is the distinction between literal meaning and strategy. Other aspects become more prominent such as the relationship between agency and interaction-type, e.g., whether the participants are engaged in a task or in the exchange of ideas, as well as the frequency with which a particular speech act expression is used in different situational contexts. The focus thus shifts towards the description of functional profiles of extended units of meaning, and the description of such units in their discourse context.

3.5 Speech act idioms revisited

Sadock's theory of speech act idioms (1974) has potential for further investigation with the use of corpus resources. He argues that certain lexico-grammatical strings such as *let's* and *why don't you* are processed as idioms, i.e., they carry a different meaning than the sum of their semantic components. Sadock's (1974:98) hypothesis is that 'indirect speech acts whose pragmatic specification differs from what the surface form appears to indicate, arose when frequently associated use became encoded in semantic form.' Although Sadock did not explore the use of corpus data when he developed this theory, it is easy to see how the study of speech act expressions in a spoken corpus might lend support to Sadock's approach.

As outlined in chapter 2, a number of criticisms have been levelled against idiom theory, most of which relate to the potential multi-functionality of the same lexical string (see Levinson 1983:269). A shift in focus from the potential multi-functionality to the extraction of patterns, both in the functional uses of particular lexico-grammatical strings and in the responses they effect, could be explored as an alternative approach to this issue. What clearly exists is a functional preference for individual lexico-grammatical strings, and a corpus can be used as a resource to establish the nature of this preference. Thus, rather than abandoning idiom theory altogether, what is needed is a framework which takes into account the degree of fixedness of such phrases, together with the distributional frequency of their senses, to assess the factors which contribute to their status as idioms. Brown and Levinson (1987:269) acknowledge that certain speech act expressions might have acquired idiom status through extended usage. However, they do not propose a framework to test this hypothesis. This is where previous research on idioms and their analysis in a corpus may provide a point of entry.

Studies into formulaic language have largely focused on the lexico-grammatical aspects of multi-word units (Weinreich 1980; Cowie & Mackin 1975; Strässler 1982). Methods of identification of formulae have been developed based on broad criteria, e.g., human intuition, frequency information or semantic and grammatical properties (e.g., idioms, light-verb constructions, adjective noun collocations). A considerable amount of research in Natural Language Processing (NLP) and in linguistics draws on two definitions by Sag et al. (2002) and Wray (2002) respectively. Sag et al. define multi-word expressions (MWEs) as 'idiosyncratic interpretations that cross word boundaries (or spaces)' (Sag et al. 2002: 2). They specify further that MWEs can be classified broadly into two categories according to their syntactic and semantic flexibility, i.e., *lexical phrases* and *institutionalised phrases*. Wray (2002: 9) argues for an approach that is 'as inclusive as possible, covering any kind of linguistic unit that has been considered formulaic in any research field'. She defines the term formulaic sequence as

> a sequence, continuous or discontinuous, of words or other elements, which is or appears to be prefabricated: that is, stored and retrieved whole from memory at the time of use, rather than being subject to generation or analysis by the language grammar.   (Wray 2002: 9)

Research into formulaic sequences that includes a functional perspective has been concerned with lexicalised multi-word units (Alexander 1984; Carter 1998). Speech act idioms, such as the ones discussed in this chapter, are special kinds of fixed expressions in that they often, and sometimes exclusively, consist of grammatical words.

Idiomatization can vary in degree depending on the extent to which certain stretches of words have acquired a new meaning which is larger than the sum of their composite parts. Fernando (1996: 64) argues that the 'pure idiom is a composite unit consisting of semantically "empty" words; consequently, a new meaning – different from what the same unit would have had if each unit were not void – is now associated with the idiom.' Criteria to determine the idiom status of a combination of words, and to distinguish literal from idiomatic usage, have been extensively discussed in the speech act literature. Sadock (1974) illustrates how properties of co-occurrence, paraphrase and grammatical restriction play a major role in assessing the idiom status of a particular speech act expression. Thus, if the interrogative pronoun in *why don't you close the door* can be paraphrased, the function is likely to be that of a question (see Section 3.6.2.4.1).

Fernando (1996) discusses what she calls *interpersonal idiomatic expressions* (1996: 153). Following Halliday's classification of metafunctions (1978), these are opposed to *ideational idiomatic expressions*, which are mainly used for the success-ful transfer of information. Fernando describes *interpersonal idiomatic expressions* mainly in terms of structuring devices, such as greetings, but also mentions *common locutions* as part of this class. The term *interpersonal idiomatic expressions* is useful as it captures the difference between such speech act idioms and conven-tional idioms.

3.5.1 Speech acts in a corpus

In order to identify different kinds of speech act expressions in a corpus, it is still necessary to define a broad functional category as an organising principle. As far as suggestions are concerned, this could be a very broad descriptor, like 'putting forward a proposal for consideration' without any restriction on the response from the hearer. This definition is in line with Verschueren's (1981) view, argues that a suggestion implies that the hearer is free to decide whether or not he/she wants to act on the suggested proposition. Similarly, DeCapua & Huber (1995:120) argue that '[a]lthough advice can be seen as a type of directive, the force of the act is to-ward the receiver accepting an evaluation, an idea rather than performing an act'. Commitment can therefore only be assigned in relation to the context of the situa-tion, i.e., as the perlocutionary effect of the utterance, rather than its illocutionary force. This is why it may be more relevant to describe directive or requestive prop-erties of a suggestion, rather than to assign them to different speech act categories altogether.

The next step is to consider typical lexico-grammatical strings which realise the function of a suggestion as outlined above, and study their functional and distributional patterns in the corpus. These strings are analysed with reference to the unit of meaning of which they form the lexico-grammatical core.

As outlined in chapter 2, Sinclair (1996) uses a set of parameters for analysing 'units of meaning'. His approach is partly based on previous theories and ap-proaches which highlight the habitual co-occurrence of individual words in lan-guage use (e.g. Firth 1957), as well as the general observation of semantic and functional patterns that emerge from the study of concordance outputs. His ap-proach is of particular relevance to the study of speech act functions in different contexts and one of the analytical components in his framework, the semantic prosody of a unit of meaning, refers directly to language function. Hoey (2005) develops the concept of *pragmatic associations* of individual lexical items which refers to patterns of pragmatic functions such as the expression of vagueness for example. The way in which notions like *semantic prosody* or *pragmatic association* relate to speech act expressions has not yet been explored in any detail, and will be the focus of the remainder of this chapter.

3.6 Functional profiles of speech act expressions

As outlined above, previous work in the area of speech act theory has been concerned with building taxonomies of different speech act expressions based on formal or functional features. I have argued that it may be useful to establish 'functional profiles' of individual speech act expressions instead. If a speech act expression features a particular type of modality as one of its collocational properties for example, it can be compared to others which exhibit a similar or different pattern. The aim is to describe the formal and functional properties of various closely related speech act expressions in a corpus, and to examine whether certain forms can be related to certain functions and contexts through the patterns that emerge when they are studied in a corpus.

Clear (1987) suggests that to analyse speech act expressions, we can separate the speech act expression from the rest of the utterance following Halliday's (1973, 1978) concept of *mood* and *residue*. This procedure implies that the proposition that follows the speech act expression is relatively independent of the expression itself. With this he follows many accounts of speech act expressions which have discussed them independently of their co-text, i.e., of the lexico-grammatical choices which follow the expression (Leech & Svartvik 1994; Nattinger & DeCarrico 1989). In such accounts, the speech act expression is regarded as the core without further consideration of the textual environment. As discussed above, Sinclair (1996) found it difficult to ascribe meaning to individual words as strong patterns of co-occurrence with other words or classes of lexical items suggest that units of meaning are 'largely phrasal' (1996:82). A similar tendency might apply to speech act expressions and they should thus be studied in relation to their co-text.

3.6.1 Functional prosody

The most relevant aspect of Sinclair's framework for the description of speech act expressions is that of semantic prosody. Semantic prosodies are associations with certain lexical items which are not easily detected by intuition (Louw 1993). Louw shows how the collocates of *set in* can colour the expression in a way that portraits a negative slant on the meaning, and the expression itself becomes partly defined by this (1993:159). Semantic prosodies have been described in terms of negative or positive connotations, as in the case of the word *happen*, which mainly takes a negative prosody (Sinclair 1991).

Building on the concept of semantic prosody, the notion of *functional prosody* is here explored in relation to speech act expressions. If, as Sinclair suggests, 'the initial choice of semantic prosody is the functional choice which links meaning to purpose' (1996:88), we should be able to describe speech act expressions in terms of the patterns and distribution that they display. It should be noted, however, that a profile of speech act expressions cannot end at the level of concordance output. The vagueness or directness of a proposition often depends on the preceding discourse, for example, whether a suggestion was elicited or not. The analysis of functional profiles will therefore be continued in chapters 4 and 5 to take the discourse level into account.

A discourse level analysis is also necessary to distinguish between *reported* and *direct suggestions*. A speech act detached from the time and situation in which it was first used has to be treated differently in terms of force and commitment. It is interesting to note that some speech act expressions tend to be used more often in reported structures. When they are used in such structures, the unit of meaning may change slightly. In the CANCODE corpus there are fewer modals as collocates in reported suggestions. The frequency with which a speech act expression is used in reported structures therefore forms part of its functional prosody. If a particular expression occurs predominantly in a reported structure, this may help assess the level of directness. In reported structures there is less reason to be indirect as the suggestion usually involves people other than the ones present, as is the case in the example below:

Line		
1	<S02>	She got me to do a job for her <$G3> fencing+
2	<S01>	Yeah.
3	<S02>	+and em I **suggest to her that it's pointless putting a fence in there** because
4		<$G1>between them and the next door the next door <$G3> that way+
5	<S01>	Mm.
6	<S02>	+and it's climbing all over the fence.
7	<S01>	Oh right. Yeah.
8	<S02>	So I said to her the **best thing I would suggest she does is to plant conifers.**
9	<S01>	Yeah. <\$O9> grow quick don't they.
10	<S02>	<$O9> <$G1> <\$O9> Yeah.

This example illustrates the need for distinguishing between *direct* and *reported suggestions* as in reported suggestions the speaker is removed from the situation and the addressee of the original speech act may not be the hearer in the current interaction. The first instance of *suggest* in this extract is a narratised report of speaking. This means that it is unlikely that the original words of the speech event are being quoted (McCarthy 1998). The suggestion puts forward an idea for consideration and, only by implication, a line of action. The second suggestion is more difficult to classify in terms of speech reporting but appears to be a combination of a direct and narratised report.

The frequency of reported structures of individual speech act expression is telling. Speech reporting allows us to use more direct language, as the rules of politeness are not necessarily as important. What becomes more important in re-ported speech is the informational content, as well as the entertainment value. Reported structures, therefore, need to be studied in their own right and separate from their direct counterparts, especially where considerations of politeness and directness are at stake. Corpus evidence allows for an assessment of whether the unit of meaning of a speech act expression remains stable in reported sequences. If it does, this would be a strong argument in favour of an initial semantic approach to speech act expressions. It would suggest that pragmatic and contextual factors form part of the unit of meaning and that meaning is encoded in the semantics of the speech act expression. Hence, we do not simply 'add' downtoners such as *just* or hedges to a speech act expression depending on the nature of the proposition, as suggested by House & Kasper (1981). Rather, these are actually part of the unit of meaning of individual expressions, and it is this property which motivates the initial choice for the speaker to use it. A concordance search of the speech act verb *suggest* in the CANCODE corpus shows that its functional use does not indicate that it is a preferred way for making suggestions, but is nevertheless often used as a way of referring to the act of suggesting. This is not surprising, especially when we consider the lexical environment of this verb. Since using the verb *suggest* is a rather direct way of making a suggestion, we find that when it is used to perform their function in a direct stucture, it occurs in heavily modalised structures.

As discussed above, the functional prosody of an expression is closely linked to its collocates, and the remainder of this chapter looks at the way in which this particular component of the functional profile of a speech act expression might be studied with the use of corpus data.

Nattinger and DeCarrico (1989:128) suggest that 'just as other lexical phrases become "entrenched" for particular functions, so do those for indirect speech act functions such as requests and offers'. However, the expressions for *suggestions* in the corpus data examined do not seem to allow for as much variation as the ex-pressions discussed by Nattinger and DeCarrico for *requests* and *offers*. And, more importantly, the kind of colligational variation they allow is often directly related to the function as a speech act indicating device. The phrase *Why don't you + verb* cannot be represented by the lexical frame *Question word + neg + you + verb* when it signals a suggestion. *For what reason don't you + verb*, for example, signals a ques-tion and not a suggestion. The 'core' of this frame is *why don't you + verb (with certain – describable - collocational restrictions)*. It is thus important to include a discussion of collocational patterns in the development of possible frameworks for speech act frames. The sections below outline how collocation might be used as a criterion in the description of speech act expressions and their functional profiles.

3.6.2 Collocation

Carter (1988: 163) defines collocation as 'an aspect of lexical cohesion, which embraces a "relationship" between lexical items that regularly co-occur'. There are various ways to determine the attraction between individual lexical items, or between multi-word expressions and lexical items. Often, there is no need for statistical analysis as patterns can be obvious from the concordance output. Statistical methods tend to compare the expected frequency with which two words co-occur in a corpus with the actual frequency of co-occurrence. There are a number of problems associated with such measures, especially for low frequency items (see Woods et al. 1986). The table below uses the C-Score to analyse the attraction between speech act expressions and other lexico-grammatical items in the range of +/− 4 words of the search phrase. The C-Score is here calculated by multiplying the Mutual Information (MI) for the collocation by the Bimodal Frequency, and dividing by the total number of occurences of the collocate. The software used to calculate the C-Score is the Cambridge International Corpus and dictionary compilation system (2003).

As outlined above, traditional accounts of speech act expressions do not take much note of collocation. This further reinforces the assumption that the same form can have a number of different functions. If the patterns surrounding a particular speech act expression are taken into account, some of the ambiguity between different possible functions can be resolved, as the tendencies that emerge from the collocational patterns allow for functional disambiguation. This point is illustrated with reference to the collocations of the speech act expression *why don't you*. Table 3.1 below shows the left hand collocates of this expression in the CANCODE corpus. The negative number stands for the position in the span of the speech act expression where the collocate is most likely to occur.

The table of collocates shows that in those cases where this expression does not occur in sentence initial position, it is often used in a reported structure.

Table 3.1 Collocates to the left of *why don't you* in CANCODE

Collocate	C-Score	Main position in span
said	6.95	−1
saying	6.16	−1
keep	5.79	−4
say	5.56	−1
says	5.47	−1
don't	4.90	−1
her	4.53	−1
him	4.49	−1
you	4.08	−1
to	4.05	−1

The concordance lines below are examples of the lemma *SAY* as a collocate of *why don't you*:

```
e day and I said to her look Why don't you just go in ask them+
            And I said "Why don't you stay for tea?" and he sai
            He said Why don't you get it.
went to the meeting and said Why don't you if you're going to have al
        And as I said Well why don't you <$=> live </$=> get them l
        And so I said Well why don't you give her a ring.
And they just basically said Why don't you just go.
    <$5> And em I said to her Why don't you put <$O26> <$G?> em </$O26
            I said "Well why don't you keep it locked up around b
        And I said "Well why don't you go from here?"
 garage in <$G2> And I said "Why don't you just erm phone a garage in
        So he said to me "<$H> Why don't you get a bike </$H> like your
            <$=> And I said "Why don't you" </$=> He was taking it t
H> our counsellor said erm "Why don't you watch some like sad films
            They all said Why don't you book somewhere for you and
t back to us you know saying Why don't you have students.
right er they'll keep saying why don't you have a look er have a look
> and they keep saying to me Why don't you come down.
ence so I keep saying to her why don't you go into that field cos you
            <$1> And saying Why don't you wear longer skirts.
$2> Em you know you say Well why don't you get in touch with so-and-s
you know I'll I'll say Well why don't you come you know.
ust for a joke I used to say Why don't you study English you know lik
        <$2> Or does he say Why don't you just say.
        <$3> And I say why don't you turn try and turn it the o
used to jibe at her and say Why don't you do English and she'd say N
    He says Look he says Why don't you if you've got six hundred
        I says to him Why don't you <$=> give er li= </$=> go
    He says Look he says Why don't you if you've got six hundred
got six hundred quid he says Why don't you just give me a third of it
```

In a reported sequence, the directness of the suggestion is removed by displacement. The addressee of the suggestion is hence unlikely to be identical with the hearer of the utterance. The study of collocations can thus add valuable evidence to the description of speech acts, especially in relation to questions of agency, commitment, and 'indirectness' through reporting structures. Further collocational patterns to the right of *why don't you* and their role in functional disambiguation will be discussed below.

3.6.2.1 *Collocation and functional distribution*
The study of collocation can also be useful when it comes to establishing the overall functional profile of individual speech act expressions, especially in relation to the frequency with which they are used to perform a particular function. For example, the speech act expression *You might ...* is often described as a typical form for tentative suggestions (Leech & Svartvik 1994:168). However, if we look at a concordance output of *you might*, we find 300 instances of this speech act expression in a 2.5 million word sub-corpus of CANCODE,

of which only 34 realise a suggestion. The others are mere predictions, such as *you might not like it*, rather than suggestions. The possible extensions to the core of the expression are limited depending on the function of the stem. For a suggestion, they are *You might as well ...*, *You might want to/like to*, and some instances of *You might be able to ...*. This kind of analysis allows for the component of functional distribution and *prototypical function* to be established, and to be added to the functional profile of a speech act expression. While the speech act expression *You might...* mainly realises predictions rather than suggestions, the expression *why don't you* mainly realises suggestions rather than questions. When it does introduce a question, however, its collocates are often verbs of personal preference or desire, such as in the example *why don't you like them*.

3.6.2.2 *Collocation and interpersonal markers*

One type of collocation of speech act expressions is particularly interesting for the study of pragmatic function. Aijmer (1996:170), following Faerch and Kasper (1989:22), calls this type 'internal modifiers'. *Internal modifiers* are non-propositional lexical items such as *just, please* and *perhaps* which act as 'downtoning devices' (Aijmer 1996:177). House and Kasper (1981) propose a list of *mitigators* and *downgraders*, but these have not been studied as part of a speech act expression. The strength of attraction that exists between certain expressions and such 'downtoners' is substantial and thus cannot be ignored in the overall description. Similarly, modal auxiliaries, such as *would, will, must*, etc., as well as verbs of cognition and desire, such as *think, want* and *know*, all express speaker stance towards a proposition (see Biber & Finegan 1989a). Aijmer (1996:171) lists a number of request markers which include the downtoner *just*, such as *could you just*. She discusses the effect of such downtoners in terms of the politeness value which they add to the utterance. However, they are not seen as part of the meaning potential of the conversational routines that are used to perform a certain speech act, but rather as 'add-ons' which enforce the politeness status of the utterance. Yet, the strength of attraction between some of these markers and individual speech act expressions seems to suggest that they form part of the meaning of the expression itself, as is illustrated in the concordance output below.

```
't like C and A. Or you know why don't you just go down the market an
                       <$2> Why don't you just wait.
 Why don't you just t= </$=> Why don't you just try one off hand Jean
           <$2> <$=> Why don't you just t= </$=> Why don't yo
                 <$1> Why don't you just put loads and loads a
 garage in <$G2> And I said "Why don't you just erm phone a garage in
 don't need to work on it so why don't you just
                       <$2> Why don't you just go to bed and shut up
   <$1> <$E> laughs </$E> Why don't you just say <$=> that you </$
 > And I thought yeah </$O25> why don't you just cut my throat FX.
```

```
         the main ones basically, Em why don't you just draw me up a list of
                          <$1> <$=> Why don't you just find a </$=>
                          <$1> Why don't you just take some stuff off?
                          <$H> Why don't you </$H> just put it on the b
e day and I said to her look Why don't you just go in ask them+
                          <$1> Why don't you just cut a slice?
                          <$1> Why don't you just keep running and we'l
                               Why don't you just go away.
                               Why don't you just leave earlier.
                               Why don't you just go to bed and lie dow
And they just basically said Why don't you just go.
got six hundred quid he says Why don't you just give me a third of it
                    <$2> Well why don't you just scrape <$X> em | them
</$=> And they go But Andrew why don't you just <$G?>.
                          <$1> Why don't you just make it easy and <$G?
  if he does but I just think why don't you just say it.
              Philip goes Oh d= why don't you just pull it off me.
                          <$1> Why don't you just find a deer and kill
                               Why don't you just say.
                               Why don't you just say.
```

The MI score for *just* as a collocate of *why don't you* is 0.66 and the C-Score is 4.64. This makes *just* a key collocate of this expression. This collocational pattern at N+1 reinforces the general function of the phrase as a whole, that of a mitigated suggestion. What seems to become evident is a tendency for 'clustering' of a number of related features which can be studied throught an analysis of collocations, and which together form part of the functional profile of this expression. The kinds of interpersonal markers which occur frequently in the close vicinity of this kind of speech act expression can be divided into modal verbs, hedges and vague language.

3.6.2.3 *Collocation and modality*

The pragmatic role of modal items, especially as mitigating devices, has received a lot of attention, especially in cross-linguistic studies (House & Kasper 1981; Blum-Kulka 1989; Faerch & Kasper 1989). House and Kasper (1981) list modals under 'play-downs' alongside past tense, progressive, negation and interrogative. A number of other realisations of modality are listed under further headings in their framework. Modal lexical verbs, such as *think* and *suppose*, are listed as 'minus committers', while modal adverbs, such as *perhaps* or *possibly* are labelled 'downtoners'. House and Kasper (1981) use the term *hedges* to refer to adverbs or adverbials, such as *kind of*, *sort of*, *just* and *really* etc., whilst they use the term *downtoners* to refer to modal adverbs, such as *perhaps*. Both are treated as 'downgraders' in their study. Others have subsumed the two under the same heading (see for example Biber et al. 1999).

Simpson (1993) uses the term *modality* to refer to those items that modify the speaker's attitude to the truth or commitment of a proposition. Those items which modify the propositional content itself will here be referred to as *hedges* and *vague language*. The notion of vague language and its associated functions has been discussed by Channell (1994). Rather than 'downtoning' the propositional content, vague language makes the propositional content less precise, using items such as *or something, and things like that* or *around*, etc. The following examples show the recurrence of vagueness in the propositions following the verb *suggest* in the CANCODE corpus. As argued earlier, we would expect that the verb *suggest* occurs frequently in modalised form, but also with vague propositions. This is borne out by an analysis of corpus data where vagueness markers occur in the majority of the 166 concordance lines of the verb *suggest*, as in the following examples.

(1)   <S01> You don't suggest that I should have highlights or a perm or *something like that*.

(2)   <S01> So I'd suggest that you looked at English Lit or History or Geography or *whatever* or Maths+ Right. +as a main module.

(3)   <S01> What I suggest you do is *just kind of erm* help yourself to *say a few like that*.

The function of modal items may here be similar to that of hedges and vague language. The pseudo-cleft construction in example (3), in combination with the hedge *just* and the vague lexical expression *kind of*, all contribute to the overall level of politeness of the suggestion. It is therefore difficult to differentiate between the exact functions of the individual devices. While they convey the speaker's stance towards the utterance, they also encode the speaker's stance towards the addressee. Finally, they are also part of the 'unit of meaning' of the speech act verb *suggest*.

The frequent use of modals in the environment of *suggest* (*would* is one of the main collocates) not only indicates a certain stance towards the proposition that follows, but also shows that the speaker tries to lessen some of the accountability that comes with this speech act when it is introduced with the verb *suggest*. In the CANCODE corpus, this slant to the functional prosody of *suggest* is further enforced by the recurrent use of constructions in which the speaker expresses or

Table 3.2 Collocates of *suggest* in CANCODE

Collocate	C-Score	Main position in span
would	6.72	−1
that	3.78	1
perhaps	3.38	2
to	3.26	−1
anyone	2.90	−3
you	2.71	2
seems	2.53	−2

evaluates the grounds for putting forward a suggestion, such as *evidence to suggest, feasible to suggest* and *logical to suggest*:

```
not see a lot of evidence to  suggest that we've achieved a total conc
$=> I think it's feasible to  suggest that perhaps <$=> y= you sh= you
ey would be a little rash to   suggest a particular time period with th
s </$=> it's logical then to   suggest that the staff will share this v
I think what we're trying to   suggest is that we don't really want a t
t you know Woolf's trying to   suggest is that you know she <$H> does l
          <$4> But I venture to  suggest that the move of throwing away e
                 I wish to  suggest simply that to understand right
sus and all he stands for to   suggest that homosexuals could ever be n
I think as you quite rightly   suggest to take it back to the world of
```

Multi-word expressions that signal reference to generic truths such as *there is evidence to suggest* for example, de-personalise the force of the speech act and allow the speaker to distance themselves from the imposition that a relatively direct suggestion would normally carry. An analysis of statistically derived collocations thus has to be complemented by a close study of the concordance output, to capture such patterns which further add to the functional profile of the speech act expression.

3.6.2.4 Collocational patterns of *why don't you, why don't we* and *why not*

Following the outline of the different aspects of collocation which seem to be of key importance for the profile of speech act expressions, the following sections provide a sample analysis of the collocational patterns of three speech act expressions: *why don't you, why don't we* and *why not*. The expression *why don't you* has already been discussed to some extent earlier in this chapter, but is used here again to highlight its profile in contrast with *why don't we*, an expression which is functionally related but semantically different.

3.6.2.4.1 *Why don't you*

The speech act expression *why don't you* can be used literally, i.e., to pose a question probing for a reason implied by the 'why' element, or it can be used to put forward a suggestion, both in a reported and direct structure. There are 182 instances of this expression in the CANCODE corpus.

A closer inspection of *why don't you* in the corpus shows that this expression is predominantly used to put forward a suggestion. In order to separate the question sense from the suggestion sense, a substitution test as used by Sadock (1974) has been applied. Thus if the 'why' element can be substituted by a lexical string with similar meaning, such as *for what reason*, this would indicate a literal meaning. Further, if the negation of the phrase was reversible, then the literal meaning was foregrounded. The following example illustrates this difference:

Line		
1	<S01>	That's elastic scattering yes that's why the sky is blue and so on.
2	<S02>	But **why don't you** get Compton scattering?
3	<S01>	Look at that equation.
4	<S02>	<$?> It's cos its energy's quite low.

In this example the speech act can only be a question. The expression is substitutable and the negation reversible.

The discourse context in which a speech act expression is used gives further indication as to its function. Suggestions can elicit responses which range from minimal acknowledgement tokens to agreement, or evaluations of the suggestion itself. Questions introduced by *why don't you*, on the other hand, require a more detailed 'answer'.

Line		
1	<S01>	**Why don't you** eat meat Sue?
2	<S02>	Because I'm an awkward git.
3	<S01>	Mm.
4	<S02>	Yeah.
5	<S01>	But **why don't you eat meat**? laughs
6	<S02>	But why do you pick out the bits on the plate and +
7	<S01>	laughs
8	<S02>	Cos I don't know. I gave up eating meat when I was about fourteen cos a friend
9		did and I was easily led by my peer group.

In the example above, speaker 1 poses a question which speaker 2 does not answer sufficiently. The 'why' element retains its full meaning, and needs to be addressed in terms of a concrete explanation. The reply offered by speaker 2, however, does not meet these requirements. Speaker 1 then repeats his question and, going back to the actual recording, we see that in the utterance in line 5, the main stress is on 'why'. Using this kind of intonation, speaker 1 emphasises that he intends his utterance to be interpreted as a question, to which he expects an answer. Speaker 2 eventually provides the answer in lines 8–9. The concordance output of *why don't you* gives rise to a particular pattern when the expression is used to introduce a question, as illustrated in the output below:

```
        <$?> Why don't you eat fish?
         But why don't you eat meat?
             Why don't you eat meat Liz?
        <$2> Why don't you ever come and see us for G
         But why don't you get Compton scattering?
   He said Why don't you get it.
        <$1> Why don't you like it Sal?
```

```
                                Why don't you like it when the big boys
                                Why don't you like them?
  What are you trying to hide   why don't you want him to stay in.
                       <$3>     Why don't you want it on a Friday?
               <$1> But         why don't you want to admit?
              <$2> "Well        why don't you want to get dressed?"
                       <$2>     Why don't you like <$G?>?
                       <$1>     Why don't you like it Sal?
                                Why don't you like it when the big boys
                                Why don't you like them?
                       <$1>     Why don't you believe in it?
     So <$=> why don't </$=>    why don't you have to ask <$073> them </
```

The instances of the speech act expression *why don't you* in the output above co-occur with a particular set of verbs. This supports their functional prosody of a question rather than a suggestion. In three of the instances, the expression is preceded by *but*, signalling disagreement, or at least a probing move. More importantly, however, are the clusters of deontic modality to the right of the expression. Most of these items express wants, likes, or obligations. As such, when *why don't you* introduces a question, it tends to question personal dispositions and preferences. Therefore, it may not be surprising that the majority of instances are found in the *intimate* and *socio-cultural* category of the CANCODE corpus. Here speakers are most off-guard and more comfortable to ask this kind of question.

When *why don't you* is used to introduce a suggestion, the collocations to the right of the expression are distinctly different from the ones that occur when it is used to introduce a question. Most notably, there is a very strong pattern with the downtoner *just* in the slot directly adjacent to the right of *why don't you*. Table 3.4 shows the main collocates to the right of this expression at N+1.

The collocation output shows that the expression *why don't you* is regularly followed by a group of transitive verbs such as *ask*, *get*, *tell* and *use*. These are also among the most frequent verbs in the English language. *Ask* and *tell* imply further verbal action involving another person. This, in turn, gives rise to a

Table 3.3 The top 10 collocates to the right of the speech act expression *why don't you* at N+1

Collocate	C-Score
just	7.36
ask	7.09
get	7.06
come	6.62
go	6.51
use	6.30
eat	6.16
tell	5.92
do	5.72
give	5.46

Table 3.4 Collocates to the right of the speech act expression *why don't you* at N+2

Collocate	C-Score
Him	4
It	3.39
Them	3.24
Your	2.99
Her	2.37

particular focus of the suggestions introduced with this speech act expression. Another prominent group of collocates are personal pronouns, such as *him, her* and
them which habitually occur at N+2 in the concordance output (see Table 3.4 and
concordance output below).

```
                         <$2> Why don't you get her something?
                              Why don't you beep her.
        And so I said Well why don't you give her a ring.
                         <$1> Why don't you give him a ring?
                         <$3> Why don't you ask him?
                         <$3> Why don't you get him to do some tapes f
                              Why don't you tell him to stop?
              <$?M> Oh. Why don't you ask him.
                         <$1> Why don't you keep it a bit longer like
                         <$2> Why don't you do it?
                              Why don't you pour it in there to check.
                         <$4> Why don't you write it down dear.
                         <$2> Why don't you put it there and have It a
                         <$3> Why don't you have it in the Lake Distri
                              Why don't you do it between phone to pho
            <$2> Well why don't you take it out and put it in
     <$1> Then then again why don't you get it in lamb?
                         <$1> Why don't you have it on top of that the
  nstead of doing it like that why don't you do it like that.
                              Why don't you save it until tomorrow or
          I said "Well why don't you keep it locked up around b
                         <$2> Why don't you wash them down like you ma
                         <$1> Why don't you give them a ring at Lancas
                         <$2> Why don't you tell them to come and mend
                              Why don't you get them out?
```

The collocations discussed above would suggest the following pattern for the
speech act expression *why don't you: Why don't you + (downtoner) + frequent verb
from set (sometimes describing another speech act) + (3rd person pronoun).* In terms
of the functional profile of this speech act expression, the corpus evidence suggests that its prototypical function is that of a suggestion rather than a question,
as summarised in Figure 3.1. The distribution of this expression across speaker
relationships is also shown in Figure 3.1. It should be noted that due to the variation in word count in the different categories, not much can be assumed about the
contextual associations of this expression based on this data. However, chapter 4

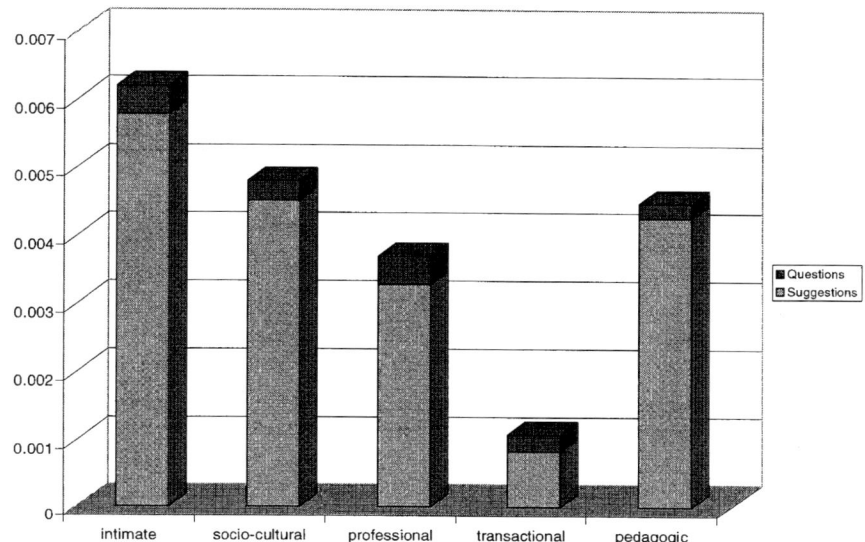

Figure 3.1 Prototypical function of *Why don't you* according to speaker relationship category in CANCODE

will deal in more detail with contextual distributions of individual speech act expressions and discuss the impact of normalisation of individual categories in small corpora.

Following the summary of the different components of the functional profile of *why don't you*, a few examples of this expression in the corpus will be discussed further. As outlined above, the expression *why don't you* is inherently direct, both from a semantic and from a pragmatic perspective. Semantically, it includes the addressee in the expression, and pragmatically, it challenges the current behaviour of the addressee by proposing a certain line of action. The direct nature of this expression creates a dramatic effect in recounts, while at the same time it does not impose on the immediate hearers, as recounts usually involve other people. The example below illustrates this point:

Line		
1	<S02>	And I I <$G?> and he kept trying to get off with me and I <$H> couldn't bear to
2		</$H> talk to him. I just completely ignored him and <$G?> keep calm <$G?>
3		and it seemed to be working. And he actually invaded my space and started
4		pointing at me literally. You know he invaded my space. <$=> I just sort </$=>
5		I just turned round and said Look. **Why don't you just go away. Why don't**
6		**you fucking leave me alone.** And he went completely mental. <$G?> completely
7		changed.
8	<S01>	What happened?

Speaker 2 in this extract recounts a personal episode, and uses the speech act expression to introduce directive force to the suggestion. This force manifests itself not only through the previous discourse, but also through the very direct proposition and expletive that is being used here. Another effect of reported suggestions which include this speech act expression is humour, as the following examples illustrate:

1)   <S02> Cos they had the Johnny Walker Tournament about a week after we left. And we were there on the beach more or less all the time rubbing shoulders with all the golfers and all the German millionaires and this one here keep telling me <$=> I should <$E> laughs </$E> </$=> Mummy **why don't you chat up one of those men over there.** They've got lots of money. <$E> laughs </$E> <$E> laughs </$E> <S02> She's a right little madam she was. Oh my God. Excuse me a moment Darling.

2)   <S02> And I said Well I'm having a rest I'm tired. Well you shouldn't go to work so much. You should stay home with me. And I thought yeah why don't you just cut my throat FX. <$E> laughs </$E>

The extralinguistic information tag, *laughs*, is one of the main collocates in the reported suggestions introduced with this expression. This highlights the creative use of the speech act expression *why don't you* in reported structures.

3.6.2.4.2 *Why don't we*

The speech act expression *why don't we* is similar in use to *why don't you*, although it does not tend to occur as a question. The inclusive pronoun *we* make this expression unsuitable for conveying a questioning force as it would entail that the speaker expresses uncertainty about his or her own position. There are two examples in the concordance output below which arguably carry a question function: *But* **why don't we** *get it* and **Why don't we** *get Compton scattering of.* However, the use of *we* in these examples is depersonalised, and the main focus is on the task at hand.

With 30 instances, *why don't we* occurs less frequently in the CANCODE corpus than the other expressions discussed in this chapter, and it is here discussed merely to point out differences with the closely related expression *why don't you*. Out of the 30 occurrences, 9 are part of reported structures. This is a similar ratio as with *why don't you*.

The collocational patterns of *why don't we* differ from those of *why don't you* in a number of respects. While there is some overlap, this expression does not regularly co-occur with the same verbs as *why don't you*, nor does it collocate with the extralinguistic marker *laughs*, which suggests that it is used for a different purpose. However, it retains the downtoner *just* as a main collocate. Given the overall low frequency of this expression, it is difficult to make any statements about possible patterns, collocational or otherwise.

However, despite the small number of instances, one of the emerging patterns seems to be that the propositions introduced by *why don't we* tend to describe relatively concrete actions, rather than further speech acts, as is the case with *why don't you*. There are a couple of examples where the expression is followed by *tell* and *ask*, as can be seen in the concordance output below.

```
              So I said to Sarah why don't we come to New York with you f
no why why don't we s= </$=> Why don't we do this.
                            Why don't we use that.
ng to send it off but listen why don't we just find pieces of plastic
ays saying For Christ's sake why don't we leave earlier+
around and they thought Well why don't we have a look in the church c
            <$2> So well why don't we just go down there now and
                <$2> Why don't we give them to somebody who m
                <$1> Why don't we have like a middle bag in t
                But why don't we get it.
        <$E> pause </$E> Why don't we get Compton scattering of v
                    Why don't we tell the press if this is r
    <$5> <$H> Then why don't we ask. </$H>
er you want to call them say Why don't we look at it.
    <$1> <$=> Why no why why don't we s= </$=> Why don't we do th
            So thought why don't we do one.
                <$3> Why don't we actually make a model of th
        <$3> Well why why don't we just change that.
            <$=> Why don't we buy a </$=> So we bought ou
                    Why don't we let the G Ps know that.
            Hey why don't we just s= do a swap.
    <$1> Yes well why don't we have a look at something el
        <$3?> <$=> Why don't we do </$=> Yeah.
or any developed system then why don't we get her to actually er anal
rge forms all the time s= so why don't we have a rubber stamp with ou
                    Why don't we just empty this out on the
        <$2> <$=> Why don't we go to </$=>
daughter young daughter said why don't we celebrate Divali with her d
            <$3> But why don't we go and just tip it in the w
            <$1> Why don't we go and find out.
```

In the corpus, there is one instance in which *why don't we* is used in 'reflective mode'. This means that the proposition precedes the expression, as shown in the following example.

Line	
1	<S03> Yeah. I I think it it's you know quite a powerful thing that's <$H> there </$H>.
2	<S01> <$=> Why no why **why don't we** s= </$=> **Why don't we do this.**

In this extract, students are preparing a debate, and speaker 3 has just suggested a way of integrating a particular focus into the discussion. Speaker 1 completes the initial suggestion in a supporting move which serves a summarising function and structures the discourse in a way that allows the participants to move on to the next topic.

The level of vagueness of the propositions that follow *why don't we* is not so much a product of face concern for the hearer, but related to the nature of the task that is to be completed. The benefit of these suggestions cannot be assigned to any of the participants directly, but rather to the task at hand, an outside cause or organisation.

3.6.2.4.3 *Why not*

The semantics of the expression *why not*, as is the case with the other expressions discussed so far, mark it as a question or an indirect speech act. In comparison to the other expressions, *why not* is the speech act expression which is most likely to function as a question in the CANCODE corpus. However, a closer look at the kinds of questions that are introduced by *why not* shows a strong resemblance to some of the functional properties of a suggestion.

There are three main functions of *why not* in the CANCODE corpus. The first one is a primary suggestion, as in the following example:

Line	
1	\<S03\> Outstanding lodgements.
2	\<S01\> **Why not just put outstanding ledgers then you know.**
3	\<S03\> No.\<$=\> I t= \</$=\> What you should put down there is outstanding lodgements.

In this example *why not* co-occurs with the downtoner *just* and the interpersonal marker *you know*. The suggestion sense of *why not* tends to follow the pattern *Why not + VP (with paradigmatic restrictions)*.

The second usage of *why not* in the corpus is a way of voicing the process of considering a line of action – almost like an interior monologue – a function that is not realised by the other speech act expressions discussed in this chapter.

Line	
1	\<S06\> Yes. Really if there's people already living there+
2	\<S01\> Mm.
3	\<S06\> +it would assure people to go there wouldn't it and people to think Well there's
4	other people living there it's all right for me.
5	\<S02\> And there's no harm come to them so **why not**.

This type of reflective mode can be related to the utterance of another speaker, or to the speaker who uses the expression. The extract above is an example of the latter. Here, the speakers develop a suggestion collaboratively, which is reinforced by the speech act expression *why not*. The position of this expression is important in this context as it appears after the proposition itself and, in the example above, after giving a supporting reason for the proposition. While this suggestion is developed collaboratively, it ascertains the autonomy of the speaker. Hence, by using the expression in this rhetorical way, the speaker maintains a dialogue which takes his or her views into account. While this use of *why not* is similar to the suggestion sense introduced above, its place in the utterance and its anaphoric point of reference create a new unit of meaning which serves a different function.

The third usage of this expression is that of introducing a question. Here the speaker probes for the reason behind in the 'why-element' of the expression. As such, it can be broken down into its composite parts and the 'why-element' can be substituted with other question forms, such as *for what reason*. Similarly, other substitution tests, such as those discussed by Sadock (1974) support the question form of this expression. The question put forward tends to challenge the content of a previous proposition, as the following example illustrates:

Line		
1	<S02>	You're not capable of knowing.
2	<S01>	**Why not?** Why the fuck aren't I capable of knowing?

While the main semantic and functional properties of the speech act expression *why not* are represented in all of the three different uses, the concept of prototypical function is worth considering further. In the case of *why not*, the main functional use in the CANCODE corpus is that of a *reflective suggestion*, and as such it entails properties of a suggestion and properties of a question, since the speaker 'consults' himself or herself. The different senses of *why not* have been determined partly on the basis of substitution tests, and also according to prosodic patterns, following consultation with the original recordings that form the basis for the transcriptions. The overall functional distribution of this speech act expression is shown in Table 3.5.

The functional profile of *why not* is supported by the collocational patterns in the data. Table 3.6 shows the strongest patterns at N–1 and N+1, with *I don't see why not* and *why not just* occurring as commonly used expressions. As discussed above, the expression *I don't see why not* signals a collaborative speech act, whereby the suggestion is developed by either the speaker or by one of the other speakers, and this expression reinforces agreement with the suggestion.

Table 3.5 The overall functional distribution of *why not* according to speaker relationship category in CANCODE

	Intimate	Socio-cultural	Professional	Transactional	Pedagogic
Suggestion	24	34	17	24	5
Question	38	43	5	6	14

Table 3.6 Collocational patterns of *why not*

Collocate	Position	C-Score
See	−1	5.77
use	1	4.65
don't	−2	4.51
put	1	4.12
said	−1	4.10
Just	1	4.08

Another strong collocational pattern lies in the co-occurrence with *just*, i.e. *why not just*, which always signals a suggestion function. The downtoner *just* is a key collocate, and the propositions introduced by this expression are very concrete, as the following examples show.

```
                          Why not just make gradual amendments to
                          Why not just say And here is The News.
            <$3> So why not just change that+
hey're gonna say to you Well why not just put the loans and should th
                   <$1> Why not just put outstanding ledgers the
       <$=> Do erm </$=> Why not just have a screen there and hav
```

It could be argued that, in the absence of agency markers in the semantics of the expression, the focus of this type of suggestion is on the action itself, rather than on commitment and benefit which, as a result, has to be more concrete. The functional prosody of a speech act expression therefore influences to a certain extent the proposition that follows. This is illustrated in the following three examples:

1.

Line		
1	<S01>	Right.
2	<S02>	So why not focus if you like the skills and develop the skills of nursing and
3		paramedic support around that patient. So we are literally inside an envelope
4		of over a hundred beds. We've tried to create again little enclaves. <$O25> <$=>
		of </$=> </$O25>
5	<S01>	<$O25> Yeah. </$O25> I had a walk round er with FX <$O26> this </$O26>
6		morning. <$=> and </$=>

2.

Line		
1	<S01>	Why not identify examples of repetition and see if you can actually categorize
2		them into different categories you know+
3	<S02>	Yeah.
4	<S01>	+across the texts and within the texts.
5	<S02>	Yeah.

3.

Line	
1	\<S02> I would agree to that wholeheartedly. Yes I think that's an excellent way of getting
2	\<$G?> We've got a good local paper **why not use it.**
3	\<S01> Mhm. Which would have both \<$O92> the positive and the negative comments \</$O92>.

As the examples above show, the proposition introduced by *why not* tends to be specific but is not necessarily tied to a particular time frame. In those instances where *why not* introduces a suggestion in the CANCODE data, it is usually followed by a non-finite verb. Often *why not*, as is the case in the last of the examples above, is used in the context of expressing a negative attitude about a third party.

The main function of *why not* in the data, however, is as a challenge in conversation or as a reflective suggestion. As such, it can have a converging, as well as a provocative, function. When it is used as a direct suggestion, the same applies. The high frequency of the challenging question function, in the *intimate* and *pedagogic* category reflects the contextual constraints. The speaker relationship in the former does not warrant a high degree of politeness and in the latter is based on an institutionally recognised level of power relations.

To summarise the findings so far, *why not* changes its collocates and its place in discourse according to the function it fulfils. Unlike *why don't you* and *why don't we*, this expression does not explicitly involve the speaker or hearer in the proposition, thus allowing for a more tentative speech act function. Often, the proposition is related to wider issues or third parties.

3.7 Summary

This chapter has explored the status of speech act expressions as a possible unit of analysis. Following a general account of how the use of corpus data might aid the development of an analytical framework of speech act expressions, some of the possible parameters of such a framework have been outlined. These parameters combine to form the functional profile of speech act expressions. The functional profile consists of collocation, functional distribution and contextual distribution of individual speech act expressions. The first two of these parameters have been discussed in this chapter, and the notion of *contextual distribution* will be further explored in chapters 4 and 5.

In this chapter I have illustrated how the analysis of collocational patterns can serve as an approach to distinguish between different functions realised by the same speech act expression. For example, in the data that was analysed, the expression *why don't you* has different collocates depending on whether it is used to introduce a question or a suggestion. The analysis of collocation further contributes to the description of speech act expressions in terms of their patterns of use in direct versus reported constructions. This part of the functional profile of an expression is a key element in the assessment of wider socio-pragmatic properties, such as the level of directness and force associated with a particular expression.

However, there are a number of limitations with the approach outlined in this chapter. Firstly, larger spoken corpora need to be examined to establish more robust functional profiles of the speech act expressions discussed here. The analysis in this chapter is only meant to be indicative of how speech act expressions might be described on the basis of corpus evidence.

Secondly, while contextual distribution is taken into account in the description of speech act expressions, it is difficult to make any generalisations about the overall level of directness. This is because context as a concept is far more complex than the basic categorisation scheme applied to the CANCODE corpus may imply. A corpus-based analysis of speech act expressions cannot therefore end at the level of concordance analysis. It has to take into account the overall context in which an utterance takes place, and recognise that this context is essentially dynamic in nature. Possible approaches to the description and analysis of context, and whether it is possible to design a corpus-based framework that would allow contextual information to become part of the functional profile of a speech act expression will be explored further in chapters 4 and 5.

CHAPTER 4

Pragmatic functions in context

4.0 Introduction

The analysis in Chapter 3 has shown how corpus evidence can contribute to descriptions of pragmatic functions in a way that would not be possible otherwise. So
far, patterns at the level of collocation and functional distribution have been discussed. One further component which contributes to the overall functional profile
of a speech act expression is the frequency with which it occurs in a particular
context.

This chapter explores further the relationship between speech act expressions
and context. The relationship between individual speech act expressions and their
use in specific discourse situations, is an area of research that has not yet been explored in detail with the use of corpus evidence. In this chapter a possible approach
will be outlined drawing on the 5 million word CANCODE corpus.

As discussed in Chapter 2, spoken corpora which have been designed according to pre-defined contextual categories may provide a useful empirical basis for
studying contextual distributions of speech act verbs and speech act expressions.
In this chapter, I will first outline a way in which the contextual categories in a
spoken corpus might be used to establish an additional component of the functional profile of a speech act expression. The value of using contextual categories
implicit in the design of spoken corpora will then be discussed in the light of existing models and theories about the relationship between lexico-grammar and
context. It will be argued that contextual categories used for the purpose of corpus
design may be too broad, and that a more fine-grained framework of analysis and
categorisation is required to capture the dynamic nature of context and associated
parameters such as participant goals, for example.

4.1 Functional profiles and corpus-design

One of the properties of functional profiles of speech act expressions is their frequency of occurrence in different contexts. The notion of absolute politeness as
suggested by cost/benefit scales in invented contexts is not necessarily an ade-
quate reflection of what is appropriate in particular situations. What may be a

polite speech act expression between work colleagues may be too stilted in intimate conversations. Traditional approaches to the description of speech act expressions tend to stop at an initial list which relates form to function, with associated values of politeness.

Most spoken corpora contain some contextual meta-data which make it possible to study particular words and phrases according to the categorisation scheme that has been applied. As outlined in previous chapters it is important to note that the results of the analysis, and thus the robustness and validity of the functional profile of a speech act expression, has to be judged in relation to the design decisions that have influenced the development of the corpus resource.

The categorisation of different speaker relationship configurations in the CANCODE corpus makes it possible to classify speech act expressions in terms of their prototypical occurrence in different contexts, rather than intuitively assigning face threatening attributes to individual lexical items (see also Adolphs 2006). In the CANCODE data, the speech act expression *why don't you*, for example, is the most frequent expression in the *intimate* category realising a suggestion, compared to the expressions *why not* and *why don't we*. This suggests that *why don't you* is a preferred expression to be used in close relationship encounters. Figure 4.1 shows the absolute frequency of different speech act expressions which realise suggestions in the *intimate* category. The figure also indicates the pragmatic functions of the different speech act expressions, where the dark grey part in the bars illustrates realisations of question functions, and the light grey part marks instances where the expression is used to make a suggestion.

Comparisons, such as the one illustrated in Figure 4.1, can be useful in describing speech act expressions in terms of their formality. Rather than making intuitive statements about the abstract formality of individual lexical items or multi-word expressions, the issue of appropriateness is foregrounded here.

The correlation between levels of politeness as encoded in linguistic choices and the relationship that holds between the speakers has been discussed extensively in previous research (Brown & Levinson 1987; Levinson 1983; Leech 1983). Spoken corpora, which are categorised in terms of the relationship that holds between speakers, allow for the unit of analysis to include this type of contextual information in the description of speech act expressions.

Figure 4.2 illustrates the distribution of the speech act verb *suggest*. We would expect that relatively direct expressions, such as *why don't you* and *suggest*, occur frequently in the most intimate encounters as issues of politeness become less pressing when the speakers have a long-standing relationship with one another.

Due to the difference in size in the different speaker relationship categories, the figures in 4.2 are given as a percentage of the total word count in each category. The absolute frequencies are given in Table 4.1.

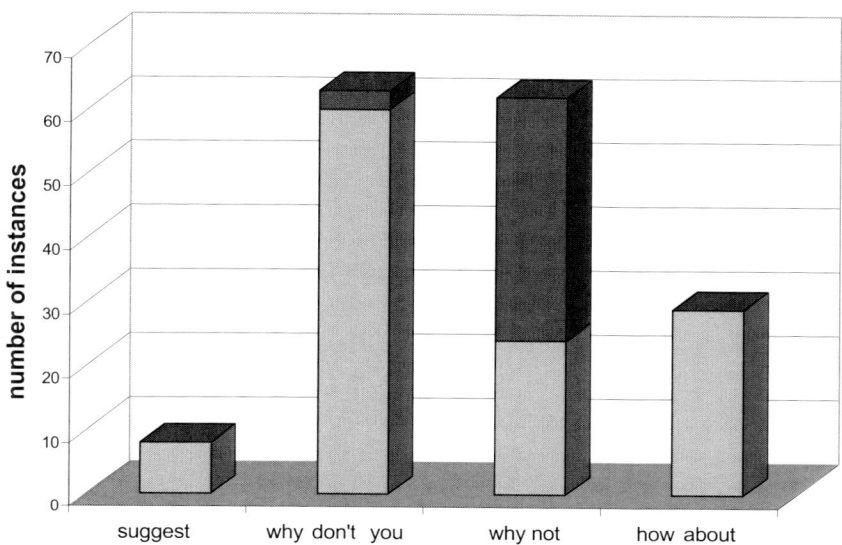

Figure 4.1 Absolute frequency of different speech act expressions and their function in the *intimate* category in CANCODE

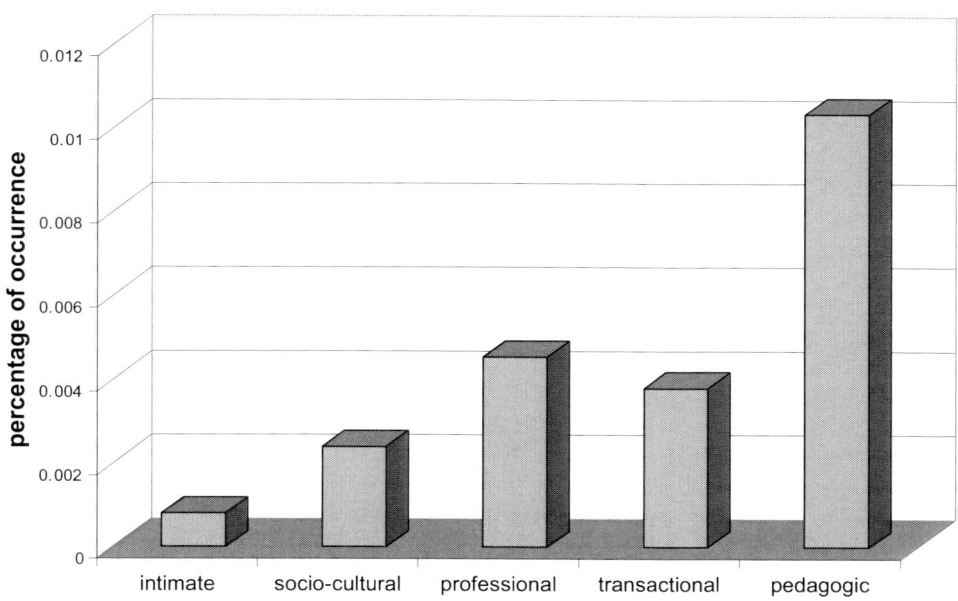

Figure 4.2 The relative distribution of the speech act verb *suggest* according to speaker relationship categories in CANCODE

Table 4.1 Absolute frequency of the speech act verb *suggest*

Intimate	Socio-Cultural	Professional	Transactional	Pedagogic
8	42	22	45	49

In terms of relative frequency, the verb *suggest* is most closely associated with the *pedagogic* category, followed by the *professional* category. This is not surprising, as we would expect a great deal of discourse in these categories to be made up of speech acts such as *suggest, advise,* etc. However, on closer examination, we see that in the *pedagogic* category, almost half of the instances introduce an idea rather than a line of action. Another 10 occur in reported structures. Despite the low number of instances of this verb in the data, such patterns may indicate that *suggest* is not a preferred verb to introduce a suggestion in the *pedagogic* category in this corpus. A similar pattern can be observed in the *socio-cultural* and *transactional* category.

The use of the verb *suggest* in the *professional* category, on the other hand, shows that all instances of this verb are suggestions which propose a line of action. None of these are reported, which could indicate that the use of the verb *suggest* to propose a line of action is an acceptable choice in the *professional* category of this data set but not in other categories. Thus, there is a context-dependent slant to the functional profile of this speech act verb. The remainder of this chapter is concerned with exploring further how the notion of *context* may be included as a component in the description of functional profiles of speech act expressions.

4.2 Text and context

There are a number of different ways in which to approach the analysis of text in relation to context. At the broadest level, a distinction can be made in relation to the direction of the research, i.e., whether it starts with contextual or textual categories. Contextual categories, such as the perceived distance between the speakers, age, class, or sex, may be considered as variables which affect linguistic variation (Goffman 1964:133). Such variables are often used as organising categories according to which texts are chosen and linguistic choices are studied. A more text-based view, on the other hand, starts with the linguistic choices in a given text or collection of texts, often with a view to highlighting their association with a particular context. Sinclair (1992:82) argues, for example, that we can expect

> the text to supply everything necessary for its own interpretation; what we need is not an external knowledge base but a better understanding of text structure. If we do not rely on the text itself to indicate its own interpretation, then we invoke mysterious processes for which it is difficult to find evidence.

The first view is based on the distinction between text internal and text external criteria, and echos the traditional division between syntax, semantics and pragmatics, whereby speech acts 'belong in a separate 'pragmatics' of utterances in their contexts-of-use' (Thibault & Van Leeuwen 1996:561). The interpretation of a speech act in this model relies on inferred meaning in context and is not seen as an integral part of the text itself.

There are a number of different approaches to the analysis and description of contextual categories. The term *genre* has emerged over the past 20 years as a powerful tool in language description, as well as in areas of applied linguistics, such as the language pedagogy (see Hammond & Derewianka 2001). The description of 'a genre' is not straighforward and various approaches have been suggested with regard to possible categories of definition. Hasan (1985), for example, sees genre in relation to semantic choices in texts. She argues that

> the statement of genre specific language is best given in terms of the semantic categories, rather than the lexico grammatical ones, since (1) the range of meanings have variant realisation; and (2) the more delicate choices within the general area are not a matter of generic ambience. (1985:113)

Others differentiate between 'genres' and 'text-types' (Biber & Finegan 1986). *Genre* in this model is defined on the basis of text external criteria, i.e. recognisable discourse genres, such as 'adventure fiction' or 'press reviews', while text-types are based on lexico-grammatical features derived with the use of statistics and text mining procedures. One of the issues with this approach, which has already been discussed in the previous chapter, is the over-reliance on categories applied to whole texts. This means that it cannot easily account for the dynamic and emergent character of context, especially where unscripted spoken interaction is the object of study.

McCarthy (1998) captures part of the dynamic aspect of discourse structure by checking texts for *goal-types*. *Goal-types* are related to the activity that the speakers are engaged in and are often manifested in the structure of texts, in that a goal-type such as 'providing information' will be reflected at a discourse level as unidirectional. McCarthy analyses a number of linguistic concepts, such as *deixis* and *formulations*, in a set of CANCODE texts, and finds that

> extracts controlled for variables such as goal type and context-type can be seen to display similarities at the lexico-grammatical level which fit in the higher-order features of generically oriented activity. (McCarthy 1998:46)

Bhatia (1993) proposes a similar approach to the analysis of texts which takes into account lexico-grammatical features, text-patterning and an interpretation of text structure.

There are thus different ways of approaching the relationship between text and context, some involving the analysis of lexico-grammar, and others relying on goal-types and folk understanding of contextual categories as clues to generic activity. The approach taken in this study combines these two methodologies in an analysis of speech act expressions in discourse.

4.3 Lexico-grammar, speech acts and context

The main concern of research on 'frames' (Aijmer 1996), 'speech events' (Hymes 1986), 'activity types' (Levinson 1992), 'speech activity' (Gumperz 1982) and 'schemata' (Cook 1994) is the description of how speakers orient themselves to a 'higher-order framework' (McCarthy 1998).

Some of the approaches that have been developed to explore the relationship between surface structures and context. Gumperz (1982), for example, discusses the use of *contextualisation cues*, a concept that describes surface features that signal 'contextual presuppositions' (1982:131). Contextualisation cues can be lexical, linguistic, paralinguistic or prosodic, and operate on different discourse levels. As such, these cues are related to the notion of 'frame' used by Aijmer (1996). Tannen (1993) also discusses linguistic features which can be seen as a realisation of the participants' orientation to a particular type of discourse. She mentions, among other features, *negative statements*, *modals* and *false starts*. These features all encode the speaker's expectations about the upcoming discourse. McCarthy (1998:32–38) discusses *expectations*, *recollections*, *instantiations* and *formulations*, and some of their linguistic realisations, as evidence of speaker goals. *Formulations* are explained as 'paraphrases of previous talk or summaries of positions reached in the ongoing talk' (1998:32). Formulations that refer to subsequent talk, on the other hand, have been described as *pre-sequences* (Levinson 1983) and meta-statements. The following extract illustrates the speaker's use of a *metastatement*:

<S01>Because **what I was going to suggest was that erm you went along to the class.**
    If if he lets you go.

Here speaker 1 introduces his/her speech act by naming it. McCarthy argues that 'suggestions by individuals are an important part of the goal-orientation and are realised both in formulaic and more indirect ways' (1998:43). Gumperz (1992) also finds that formulaic expressions at the beginning of an utterance trigger inferential processes which link the discourse to the context.

While the importance of meta-statements in this context has been recognised before (Schegloff & Sacks 1973), the role of speech act expressions has not been explored in relation to participants' interpretations of discourse, nor in relation to their expectations regarding the goal-type and text-type. They are not related to context in the routinised way suggested by Halliday, as in phrases like *once upon a time* (1985: 37) which indicate that the speaker is about to relate a fairy-tale, but they nevertheless carry generic information.

The key question that arises has been articulated by Hasan:

> can definite statements be made about the linguistic selections in a text-type that are genre motivated, so that every text belonging to a genre would display those linguistic properties?   (Hasan 1985: 108)

To address this question, Hasan discusses three texts which are structurally similar but are verbally different. She comes to the conclusion that 'it is not possible to claim that [...] if two texts are structurally identical, then they must be verbally identical [...]' (1985: 112). By building this important claim into her theory, Hasan is able to maintain that 'only certain aspects of texts are sensitive to context', which means that she 'has rejected the crude determinism whereby each text and its context are utterly predictive of each other' (ibid).

In her study, Hasan examines individual speech acts and finds that a demand, for example, can have varying lexical realisations, probably related to the relationship between the speakers. In a given genre, such as a 'service encounter', the differences in lexical form that the speech act takes do not influence or change the genre as such. However, wording must affect genre at some level as otherwise, there would be no link between the two. Hasan therefore suggests that genres are realised through meanings, or processes, which are realised through a specific class of verbs.

Hasan's rejection of a determinant relationship between verbal identity of a text and genre is based on a discussion of three short texts. This makes it difficult to ascertain whether there are any lexico-grammatical patterns which emerge from an association with a particular genre. The conclusion that may be drawn from Hasan's discussion is thus not so much that lexico-grammar is not directly related to genre, but rather, that more corpus data and analysis are needed to determine the type of relationship that might exist between the two. It is also noteworthy that Hasan starts her analysis with lexico-grammatically different entities used in a similar context. It is therefore worth exploring whether an analysis that keeps both the linguistic and the contextual variables stable might lead to a different perspective on the relationship between language and context.

4.4 Genre and text-type

As outlined in Section 4.2, the two approaches that mark the difference between text-based and context-based descriptions of recurring situations are 'text-type' and 'genre'. In the following section the notion of text-type and its role in the analysis of context will be explored. The emphasis, however, is not on determining various genres or text-types as such, but rather on the relationship between social processes, such as 'explaining', 'arguing' and 'narrating', their relation to goal-categories, such as 'decision-making', and the relationship between such social processes and context.

The terms *text-type* and *genre* are sometimes used interchangeably, however, while the term *genre* has traditionally been associated predominantly with literary conventions, the notion of *text-type* has been used in relation to textlinguistic models (see Esser 1993 for a discussion). Askehave and Swales (2001) distinguish between a text-driven and context-driven definition of genre which is associated with two different layers of analysis. While genres are generally determined on the basis of external criteria (Biber 1988) and identified by their function and communicative purpose (Swales 1990), text-types are similar in linguistic form to each other and identified by text internal criteria (Biber 1988). Genres are therefore linked more readily to culturally recognisable categories such as 'the research article' (Swales 1990), or 'fiction'. Text-types, on the other hand, are more of an analyst's category (Köster 2001), and can be described in terms of the processes they fulfill, such as arguing, discussing, etc. Genres tend to be closely related to the discourse community in which they occur (Swales 1990). Hence, certain genres, such as 'service encounters', will be defined differently by people living in different countries where the procedures and constraints of such encounters differ. The relationship between genres and text-types is maybe closest when the interaction is highly structured, such as in a 'court-hearing'. Here, the textual structures are more easily described as the genre constraints are at a maximum. The same applies for written genres, such as recipes.

The difference between genre and text-type is thus at least twofold. Firstly, text-types are based on linguistic description, while genres are often based on folk-categories. Secondly, text-types are associated with social processes while genres are associated with products. However, Harrison (2001) argues that recurrence of a particular text-type in a genre defines the genre: 'If narrative is probabilistically of high frequency in conversational argumentation, then its level of probability becomes part of the definition of the genre itself'.

For the purpose of this discussion text-types will be seen as being akin to social processes, albeit described from a different perspective. Where social processes are a general descriptive category for culturally recognised activities, 'text-types' are conceived of in terms of the structure of such processes. Similarly, goal-types, such as 'problem-solving', can be explained from the perspective of social processes, as well as from the perspective of text-type. If seen as a social process they would be related to the actual process of solving a problem and if seen as a 'text-type' they would be related to the textual structures and turn options associated with such processes. The three perspectives, goal-type, text-type and social process, represent distinct points of departure in a possible model. By combining them, it becomes possible to account for the dynamic character and structure of interactions that are associated with specific contexts.

4.5 Text-types and lexico-grammar

A quantitative approach to the study of text-types has been proposed by Biber and Finegan (1986). They analyse the one million-word Lancaster-Oslo Bergen corpus, which includes texts taken from 16 different genres, according to 41 morpho-syntactic features. Their study assumes a direct relationship between co-occurrence of linguistic features and communicative function. Biber and Finegan (1986) identify textual dimensions such as 'reported versus immediate' style.

Through statistical procedures, such as cluster analysis, Biber and Finegan arrive at nine linguistically similar text-types, such as 'immediate interaction' or 'formal exposition' (1986). The result of their analysis is that almost all genres are spread over several text-types, and all text-types contain texts from several genres. Biber (1989) therefore concludes that genres are based on a different theoretical basis compared to text-types. Again, his findings may be the result of genre mixing and text-type embedding. What is interesting in the light of the current discussion is the choice of linguistic, or morpho-syntactic, features that were used for the purpose of a general text-typology. All of the features that were used in the analysis had originally been identified as bearing some relevance for the distinction between speech and writing. Esser (1993) argues in this context that it is questionable that the same features should be relevant for a general typology. The approach proposed by Biber and Finegan (1986) differs significantly from that of Hasan (1985) in that actual linguistic items are treated as determinants for communicative purpose and thus for genre. Textual structures, on the other hand, are not taken into account.

The main difference between the approaches outlined above lies in the unit of analysis and in the direction of the research. The next section will consider these two aspects in relation to the study of speech acts and genre.

4.6 Speech acts and genre

Speech acts have always played an important part in categorising genre, as well as text-types (Longacre 1983; Hasan 1978; Dudley-Evans 1994). The stages of a certain genre, for example a 'service encounter', are realised by certain obligatory and optional elements (Hasan 1985). These are, in turn, describable in terms of speech acts. The first stage of a service encounter, for example, could be described as 'Salutation' (Mitchell 1957), realised at a speech act level as 'greeting'. Hoey (1983), in a discussion of decision-making discourse, identifies a number of lexical signals for the various stages in this type of discourse. Hence the word *problem* often occurs in the beginning of a decision-making process. While Hoey relates the use of the word *problem* to a particular stage within a specific (problem-solution) textual pattern, Gumperz (1982) argues that there are lexical formulations in discourses which reveal speaker goals (see also Craig 1990). This means that certain speech acts reveal the discourse goals of the speakers. A pre-sequence such as *I want to make a suggestion* signals the speaker's desire for his or her utterance to be understood as such. Again, no exhaustive list of lexico-grammatical features exists that is related to particular goals.

4.7 Goals and discourse

A discourse goal is identified here in terms of discourse structures and relates to the way in which participants in a conversation negotiate turns to achieve an outcome. Since conversation is inherently dynamic, such goals are transient, which means that the unit of analysis needs to be suitably restricted in length. A bottom-up approach is thus advocated which starts at the level of speech act and includes an analysis of the surrounding turns. Top-down approaches can sometimes be too inflexible to account for the relationship between lexico-grammar and context, and are also largely unable to account for the fluidity of speaker goals and the accompanying dynamic character of discourse structure.

Previous research on the relationship between speaker goals and context has shown that there is a link between contextual constraints on speaker contribution in relation to individual speech acts. Köster (2001) finds, for example, that suggestions in 'decision-making' discourse can be made by all participants while suggestions in 'advice-giving' discourse can only be made by the advice giver. While the goal of the former is to make a joint decision, the goal of the latter, according to Köster, is 'to get the addressee to carry out some action' (2001:75). Similarly, Hudson (1990), in an analysis of a gardening radio phone-in programme, differentiates between 'diagnosis texts' in which the caller is provided with a diagnosis on a previously described problem with his or her plants, and 'how to texts' in which the caller receives advice on the process of caring for a plant. Hudson finds linguistic and structural differences within the two 'text-types' which respectively follow different goals. In the same vein, Eggins and Slade (1997:235) argue that 'texts of different genres reveal different lexico-grammatical choices.'

Goal-types resemble text-types to a certain extent. Thus, the goal 'reach agreement on an issue' can be realised by the text-type 'observation-comment' (Martin & Rothery 1986). The generic activity, then, emerges from the texts themselves in the patterns that become obvious in texts of the same context-type or goal-type.

No comprehensive taxonomy of goal types exists although textual structures have repeatedly been linked to goal-directed behaviour (see for example McCarthy 1998 on decision making).

The sample analysis below starts with the speech act expression and then builds a unit of analysis around the expression. To illustrate this approach, two speech act expressions that are traditionally associated with making suggestions are analysed. The sample analysis explores the extent to which different lexico-grammatical realisations of a speech act express different goal-types. Since goal-types mirror generic activity, a relationship between lexico-grammar and goal-types would be indicative of a link between the verbal identity of a text and genre.

4.8 Sample analysis

The following sample analysis compares the discourse sequences which surround the speech act expressions *why not + Verb* and *how about + Verb*. The two speech act expressions *why not* and *how about* have both traditionally been described as suggestion markers (Leech & Svartvik 1994). In order to control the variable 'speaker relationship', only instances which are used in casual conversations be-tween close friends have been considered, and a sub-corpus of CANCODE has been designed to include only those interactions. Since the speakers are on an equal footing, any distinguishing textual patterns are therefore unlikely to be related to differences in power distribution between them.

In the CANCODE data the main functional role of both of these speech act expressions is that of a question which is different to the function investigated here. However, there are four instances in each category which introduce a suggestion. These instances are listed in the form of a concordance output below.

it </$=> you know	**why not**	sort of make it a bit m
ey want to do a job	**why not**	do it through the night
people living there	**why not**	build on the lot anyway
the police is well	**why not**	put some sort of type o
	How about	you know looking at t
	How about	we look at a situatio
<S02>	**How about**	finding out?
<$?>	**How about**	sampling a bottle of

The low number of instances of this speech act expression means that the sample analysis provided here can only serve the purpose of illustrating a possible ap-proach to the study of the relationship between language and context. However, despite the limited set of examples, it is clear that these speech act expressions are not functional synonyms. There are differences that can be gleaned relatively easily from the concordance output. While *how about* occurs in utterance initial position, the *why not* examples occur in mid-utterance. As such, we find that in three of the four *why not* examples, the speaker him or herself has stated the reason for the suggestion in the same turn preceding the suggestion. A current issue is stated followed by a suggested improvement of the situation:

Line		
1	<S02>	They'll give you twenty four hours' notice.
2	<S01>	Right.
3	<S02>	Erm we get a card saying that we're going off such and such a time twelve o'clock
4		at night and coming back on at+
5	<S01>	Mm.
6	<S02>	+six o'clock the next evening+
7	<S01>	Yeah.
8	<S02>	+you know. Erm and like my husband say he's been out and comes back at one
9		two o'clock in the morning well there's nobody up there working.
10	<S01>	Mm.
11	<S02>	Erm if they want to do a job **why not do it through the night.**
12	<S01>	Mm.
13	<S02>	They've got the lights to do it.
14	<S01>	Mm.

Here, speaker 2 is relating a current situation regarding working regulations at an electricity supplier. The goal-type in this extract is complaining or lamenting. Speaker 1 responds with backchannels. Interestingly, this suggestion is embedded in a conditional structure. Hudson argues that 'In directives, the conditional clause sets up some situation in which agency coding is an issue' (1990: 294). Agency in this extract is encompassed by people other than the speaker or the hearer. The same applies to the use of *why not* in the next extract:

Line		
1	<S01>	Right. Right. Don't you think people might go there if they were like you know
2		cheaper the prices were a bit lower or something like that.
3	<S03>	No. Why should they. You you don't want to put your life in your own hands if
4		you don't know what the hell's going on do you.
5	<S01>	There's a lot of
6	<S02>	You're lot you're not gonna find You're not gonna pay say seventy thousand pound
7		there when you can get one f= further away for the same price.
8	<S01>	Right. Well just another thought. I mean And given that this is built up already I
9		mean the area's like a lot of people living there **why not build on the lot anyway if**
10		**you already got people in the area?** I mean
11	<S03>	You can do. You you Obviously you can do. Or you can go You can go either way.
12	<S01>	Right.

Again, in this extract the participants are discussing an issue that calls for action on the part of people who are not part of the conversation. This time it is related to safety issues for housing near an industrial plant. The text-type is different, in that it has changed from recounting to discussing, which is reflected in the turn-taking structure. The turns are more evenly distributed than is the case in the previous extract. While the discussive element was advanced by only one speaker in the previous extract, it is jointly achieved in this one. This does not change the goal-type, however, which is to reach agreement on an issue by pointing out faults of other people or systems.

When we consider the instances of *how about*, a different pattern emerges at the discourse level. The use of *how about* in the examples seems to be restricted to discussions about personal 'problems'. This means that they introduce a suggestion that is aimed at improving the situation of one of the speakers. The suggestion emerges through a joint discussion, or by one speaker expressing a need for improvement of a situation. The following extract illustrates this point:

Line		
1	<S03>	I couldn't go and be a university lecturer.
2	<S02>	That is the one job prospect of doing a P H D. Are there any others?
3	<S03>	I can't think of any. Can you?
4	<S02>	Do you wanna really wanna be a university lecturer?
5	<S03>	Yeah.
6	<S02>	You do.
7	<S03>	Yeah. Be a laugh. [laughs]
8	<S02>	Er no. Do you?
9	<S03>	Yeah.
10	<S02>	More than any other job?
11	<S03>	Mm. No. Maybe. I want to what I really want to do is go and work for academic
12		publishing.
13	<S02>	Oh.
14	<S03>	That's what I really want to do.
15	<S02>	But do you need a P H D to do that?
16	<S03>	I'm not sure.
17	<S02>	**How about finding out?**
18	<S03>	Mm.

The two speakers in this extract are discussing the job prospects of speaker 3 who is considering enrolment into a PhD programme. The suggestion *How about finding out* is related directly to a problem introduced by speaker 2. As such, agency is foregrounded, as one of the speakers is directly involved. The text-type has shifted from discussion to advice giving, which is realised in a problem-solution sequence. The main goal is that of 'problem-solving' in this particular episode.

In the following extract *how about* occurs in a reported sequence, but nevertheless shares some of the features of the previous extract:

Line		
1	<S01>	Well she she'd she'd given it up. Erm+
2	<S02>	Mm.
3	<S01>	+erm+
4	<S02>	She was working out her notice.
5	<S01>	two months ago.
6	<S03>	And not having grief from her boss.
7	<S02>	Mm.
8	<S03>	But erm+
9	<S01>	But she's I mean+
10	<S03>	+the erm+
11	<S01>	+the fact that this consultancy came up
12	<S03>	+Irish cousin's taking care of
13	<S02>	Oh so she's got some work. She's got more work.
14	<S01>	Yeah.
15	<S02>	Oh great.
16	<S01>	Cos the day after she she works with various suppliers and suppliers the day after
17		this driver went and said Look. **How about you know looking at the market and**
18		**developing newer new products.**
19	<S02>	Right.
20	<S01>	I think she felt that she wasn't being very creative because+
21	<S02>	Right.
22	<S01>	+er
23	<S02>	She was just doing a day-to-day type

While this extract differs from the previous one in that the suggestion is reported, there are still similarities within the story that is being told. The reported suggestion is a response to a personal 'problem' rather than a wider issue. And since the language in narratives is partly based on the knowledge of such situations, there may be at least an indirect relationship between the direct use of the expression *how about* and the reported counterpart. The third example of *how about* highlights another possible use of this expression.

This extract is task-oriented and refers to an immediate material context. The speakers in this extract are eating a meal and one of the speakers has spilled some red wine. The process of stain removal is accompanied by comments from various speakers related to the task at hand. Towards the end, in line 6, one of the speakers makes the suggestion *How about sampling a bottle of white* which is followed by laughter. While the goal-type is somewhat different from those in the other *how about* episodes, this instance still refers to a personal problem rather than a general one.

Line		
1	\<S01\>	It's just a good thing for getting out stains
2	\<S02\>	Yeah. [laughter]
3	\<S01\>	White velour [laughter]
4	\<S02\>	And then you put salt on to get the wine out.
5	\<S01\>	That's right yeah.
6	\<S02\>	**How about sampling a bottle of white.** [laughs]
7	\<S01\>	Oh. that food
8	\<S02\>	Yes. I think it's a good idea.

The last extract is taken from the same conversation as the second *why not* example above in which the speakers discuss possible solutions for building houses close to an industrial plant. This interaction provides a useful example for illustrating the relationship between genre embedding, text-type, goal orientation and lexico-grammar.

Line		
1	\<S01\>	Well tell you what. Let's look at that situation then. Cos that's. Erm I mean we've
2		talked about an existing plant there right and about+
3	\<S02\>	Yeah.
4	\<S01\>	+putting new houses round it. **So how about the other way round. How about**
5		**we look at a situation where we're we're talking about maybe putting a new plant**
6		**into an area right.** Let's say here that we've got these two sites site A and site B
7		right which are both industrial sites.
8	\<S02\>	Mm.
9	\<S01\>	But neither of them have anything going on there at the moment+
10	\<S02\>	Mm.
11	\<S01\>	+that represents any kind of risk to the people living nearby right.
12	\<S02\>	Mm.

The text-type here is still one of 'discussing', although speaker 1 is holding the floor in this episode. The main goal type remains 'collaborative idea' but the sub-goal type has changed when compared to the *why not* episode in the same conversation from reaching agreement by 'relating faults' to 'organising discourse'. The suggestion introduced with *how about* refers to the way in which the participants 'should' organise their discussion in order to reach agreement. Again, the commitment is on the part of the participants, not on an external agent. As such, it is geared towards the notion of 'success', rather than 'understanding', as was the case in the *why not* episode taken from the same conversation.

It seems then that the corpus data used for this analysis points to differences between the two speech act expressions and their relation to genre. These come out most prominently in the type of problem that is being addressed, which in turn is related to the goal-type and to the text-type. *Why not,* for example, is mostly used to address a wider issue in the context of a discussion, with the aim of complaining or lamenting. *How about*, on the other hand, is used in suggestions directed towards an identified problem related to other participants in the conversation. The problem itself has either arisen through the situation or through a comment made by one of the speakers.

4.9 Summary

This chapter has outlined a possible approach to a corpus-based study of speech act expressions in relation to situational context. The discussion suggests that corpus evidence might be useful in making this relationship more explicit. Returning to Hasan's (1985: 114) suggestion that verbal identity and generic identity of a text are not probabilistically related, the analysis in this chapter has shown that a corpus might be able to provide evidence for a reevaluation of this claim. It has been argued that goal-types should be included in such a framework. The sample analysis has illustrated how speech act episodes might prove to be a suitable starting point in the discussion about the relationship between lexico-grammar, discourse and genre orientation. The nature of agency in such episodes is an important indicator for generic activity and is easily overlooked in the wider scheme of the generic structure of texts. However, the sample analysis presented in this chapter is based on a relatively small set of data and not too much should be claimed for it until further research has confirmed the results.

Chapter 5 will build on the discussion in this chapter to illustrate how corpus data might inform a discourse-based framework for analysing speech act expressions as part of speech act episodes in context.

Exploring pragmatic functions in discourse

The speech act episode

5.0 Introduction

The previous chapter has explored the relationship between text-types and genres, as well as between speech act expressions and context. The small-scale study that was carried out using data from CANCODE has illustrated a possible framework for analysing speech act expressions in relation to contextual categories. The analysis showed that individual speech act expressions appear to be loosely related to different goal-types in the data. Whilst *why not* occurred mainly in suggestion episodes that 'criticised' other people or systems, and was not directed towards the hearer, *how about* occurred more frequently in suggestion sequences that were concerned primarily with 'problem-solving' processes, and directed towards one of the participants in the conversation. However, to account for such a correlation between goal-type and speech act expression systematically requires a dynamic discourse analysis model that accommodates various sequential and functional choices within the speech act episode.

This chapter considers the scope of using a spoken corpus to develop a discourse-based description of pragmatic functions. Thirty concordance lines of three of the speech act expressions discussed in Chapter 3, *why don't you, why not* and *why don't we* have been used as the basis for looking at the wider discourse context in which they occur, and for developing a possible unit of analysis at the level of discourse. The chapter starts with a discussion of how existing approaches to discourse analysis might assist in the analysis of patterns at the level of discourse in a corpus of spoken English. The speech act episode is then developed as a possible unit of analysis based on examples from the CANCODE corpus. A number of key issues relating to the nature of the relationship between speech act expressions, goal-types, and discourse structure will also be addressed. The focus will be on outlining possible extensions to existing frameworks for discourse analysis to be able to account for the examples of suggestions examined in the corpus.

The approach taken in this book considers pragmatic functions from the perspective of particular lexico-grammatical strings that have traditionally been associated with specific speech act functions. Starting with a speech act expression and analysing all of its instances of use in a corpus means that there will be a number of instances which would not traditionally be classified as candidates for a particular function. For example, speech act expressions might introduce a reported suggestion or one which concerns people other than the hearer. In terms of felicity conditions such examples might not fulfil the necessary requirements for a particular function and would be classified as a different speech act. However, the stance taken here is that we need a comprehensive analysis of the way in which speech act expressions are used in discourse, and build a framework around the data that emerges from the corpus, rather than relying too much on a priori conditions. The classification of individual functions based on the speech act expression might therefore differ substantially from traditional pragmatic analyses. However, corpus-based models of description might generate new insights into pragmatic functions in use which have a stronger empirical basis, and might help re-evaluate more traditional frameworks of assigning functions to utterances.

The framework outlined in this chapter is preliminary and further corpus analysis is required to test whether it might be able to account for the different discourse patterns we find in naturally occurring data, and whether it is a useful starting point for describing the relationship between speech act expressions and goal-types.

5.1 Making suggestions: Units of analysis at the level of discourse

As outlined in Chapter 2 previous research into the description and analysis of advice-giving sequences has mainly focused on institutional contexts in which the authority between the speakers is clearly defined, either because of the context itself or because advice is explicitly being sought (Banerjee & Carrell 1988; Bardovi-Harlig & Hartford 1990; Jefferson & Lee 1992; Morrow 2006). However, in the suggestion episodes identified in the CANCODE corpus, authority is not always pre-assigned, and the advice itself is negotiated in the conversation rather than 'sought' by one speaker and 'given' by the other, as the following extract demonstrates.

In this conversation, speaker 3 is recounting an event that involves her carrying heavy bags of shopping. She is not openly seeking advice, however. Yet, both speaker 1 and speaker 2 assess the situation as problematic, and speaker 2 eventually offers advice. This piece of advice is not unsolicited but arises from the assessment of the situation. Since most of the research in this area is on advice rather than suggestions, it is included here in the discussion of suggestions. However, the difference in terms of the institutional role of advice and suggestions is

Line		
1	<S03>	You see I went to Newmarket yesterday morning and I bought a melon on <$G?>.
2	<S02>	Mm.
3	<S03>	And I thought Now why have you done that. And I bought a nice big cauli=.
4	<S02>	Yeah.
5	<S01>	Ah.
6	<S03>	And then I saw if you bought seven pound of potatoes you got seven pound for
7		nothing.
8	<S01>	Oh. Stupid girl.
9	<S03>	I know I am.
10	<S01>	You carried all that. You <$G?>.
11	<S03>	And when I got home well I just opened the door and threw it in.
12	<S01>	Well.
13	<S02>	You need <$G?>.
14	<S03>	Then two hours later my daughter came. I said "Bring that shopping through to
15		the kitchen." You're mad. You're mad. That's what you are.
16	<S01>	Yes you are.
17	<S02>	You need a nice little trolley like mine. **Why don't you do your shopping on a**
18		**Monday afternoon.**
19	<S01>	Well I think it's silly that for for you to carry that.
20	<S03>	I know but I didn't intend to buy potatoes if they weren't giving them away.

crucial, and needs to be borne in mind when comparisons with previous studies are made.

The strict division between *advice giver* and *advice seeker* (Jefferson 1984; Bardovi-Harlig & Hartford 1990), as well as that between *solicited* and *unsolicited advice* (DeCapua & Huber 1995) needs to be revised in order to accommodate the suggestion episodes discussed in this book. The various text-types are important in this context, as there are likely to be text-types other than 'advice-giving', in which suggestions are put forward.

The key aspects that have to be taken into account in the development of a possible framework for analysing suggestions are the goal-types and the related text-types, the question of agency and the resulting sequential organisation. In his 'SPEAKING' model, Hymes (1972) proposes a framework for the analysis of speech acts in context, and highlights the importance of the question of authority in a 'speech event'. This question is closely related to that of agency in that the nature of the advice depends not only on the person who issues it, but also on the addressee of the suggestion. To view speaker authority and agency as complementary allows for a more reciprocal framework in that the authority of the advisor with his or her structural options is seen in relation to the assumed 'advisee' of the suggestion.

The discussion so far suggests that the dimensions 'goal-type' and 'agency' are strongly related. However, they address different aspects of generic activity. The notion of *agency* marks the relationship between the context-type and the goal-type, and between the context-type and the text-type. In the pedagogic context-type, for example, the individual speakers are aligned in a particular way which is interactively realised in the goal-type and the text-type. A lecturer, for example, in a pedagogic context, may realise his or her authority interactively in the goal-type 'information provision' which, at the text-type level, is realised as 'lecturing'. The text-type 'lecturing' in turn, may satisfy the goal-sub-type of 'knowledge transfer'. The goal-sub-type is therefore an entity, which is related to the text-type, which in turn is realised by various 'speech act episodes'.

The third aspect of the suggestion episode which, to a certain extent realises the goal-type/ goal-sub-type and the context-type, is the sequential organisation at text-type level, which can be further broken down into episodes. The sequential properties of 'episodes' are not easy to represent in a model, as there can be a high degree of variation within such sequences. Jefferson and Lee (1992) discuss the modelling of a prototypical 'troubles-telling sequence' (1992:522) on the basis of a range of conversations. They find that even though some properties of this sequence could be detected in most of the discourse stretches they had identified as 'troubles talk', 'the actual instances of troubles talk comprised very messy versions of the candidate sequence' (1992:522). In order to identify salient features of a particular sequence, it is important to focus on a narrow set of properties rather than on all of the aspects of the sequence. The model proposed in this chapter will therefore concentrate on the issue of 'agency' and 'authority' in the description of sequences.

A unit of analysis which goes beyond the utterance or concordance output is necessary in order to fully describe individual speech acts in context. A corpus seems an apt tool to outline the different types of structures in which particular speech act expressions occur. This chapter thus explores how corpus data can be used to outline the parameters of an extended discourse based unit of analysis which in turn becomes part of the functional profile of a speech act expression.

5.2 Static versus dynamic models

In order to capture the relationship between the speaker who makes a suggestion and the person who expresses a problem – the advisor and the advisee – a dynamic framework is required which allows for different speakers to occupy different roles within the sequence. Since 'authority' is seen here not only in relation to the static roles of the speakers in context, but also as unfolding in the ongoing discourse, it is important to use a model that can account for this process. A dynamic model is concerned with describing processes rather than products. The emphasis thus changes from the 'type of exchange' to 'move options' in the exchange (see Martin 1988).

The interactive process of making a suggestion can only be represented accurately if we take into account the different speaker roles in relation to their turns in the episode. An episode in which a speaker makes a suggestion following his or her own negative assessment of a situation has to be assessed differently from a sequence in which a suggestion follows the explication of a problem by another speaker. Both are related to different goal-sub-types in that the former is more likely to aim at furthering an argument or 'getting a point across', while the latter is more likely to be related to a 'problem solving' goal-sub-type.

O' Donnell (1990:325) discusses a dynamic model to account for the various options at the level of exchange, and argues that a 'dynamic model makes salient which participant is making which structural decisions within the exchange. It is therefore possible to see who (if anyone) is primarily responsible for directing the social process.' He further points out that a 'dynamic model allows the interactive, and co-operative, nature of the exchange to become salient' (ibid).

A dynamic model is also better suited to describing the linguistic choices which are constrained by contextual variables, such as the relationship between the speakers for example, and the fluidity of structural options within the episode itself. In a comparative study of suggestions in Greek and English, Marmaridou (1988) points out that since the description of suggestions often depends on how it is treated by the co-participant, 'it is immediately obvious that this model should be process rather than product oriented' (1988:125).

The following extract illustrates this point. In contrast to a suggestion in which a speaker makes a negative assessment which is followed by a suggestion by another speaker, the speaker in the extract below is also the one who makes the suggestion which affects the turn-structural options.

In this extract, speaker 2 shares with speaker 1 her thoughts about a previous situation. She puts forward a number of negative evaluations in lines 1, 2 and 5. She is not, however, seeking advice from speaker 1, but rather proposing a possible solution herself. Thus, the text-type changes from 'advice giving' to 'criticising'. The goal-sub-type changes also from 'problem-solving' to 'making a point' or 'making the other speaker understand a situation'. The suggestion *why not do it through the night* addresses agents who are different from the participants in the conversation. This is in keeping with the structural progression, since the suggestion has not been elicited by any of the participants.

In any discussion of dynamic frameworks for corpus analysis, a cautionary note is in order. It is argued above that a dynamic framework is necessary, yet the development of the framework is based on static data. As such, certain assumptions are made regarding the perception and intention of utterances by speakers and hearers at the time of the conversation. Hence, what is classified as a 'negative

Line		
1	\<S02\>	Because the water's gotta go off. But I don't see why it has to go off the length of
2		time it does.
3	\<$?F\>	Mm.
4	\<S01\>	Mm.
5	\<S02\>	And why over night. Because there's never nobody working up there+
6	\<S01\>	Right.
7	\<S02\>	+overnight.
8	\<S01\>	No.
9	\<$?F\>	There isn't.
10	\<S01\>	Mm. So you you said n= not many people work there at night. I mean \<$=\> is it
11		it's not \<\\$=\>+
12	\<S02\>	I've never seen.
13	\<S01\>	+it's not the sort of twenty four hour type \<$H\> services \<\\$H\>.
14	\<S02\>	Well I've never seen. They they'll
15	\<S01\>	Right.
16	\<S02\>	They'll give you twenty four hours' notice.
17	\<S01\>	Right.
18	\<S02\>	Erm we get a card saying that we're going off such and such a time twelve o'clock
19		at night and coming back on at+
20	\<S01\>	Mm.
21	\<S02\>	+six o'clock the next evening+
22	\<S01\>	Yeah.
23	\<S02\>	+you know. Erm and like my husband say he's been out and comes back at one
24		two o'clock in the morning well there's nobody up there working.
25	\<S01\>	Mm.
26	\<S02\>	Erm if they want to do a job **why not do it through the night.**
27	\<S01\>	Mm.
28	\<S02\>	They've got the lights to do it.
29	\<S01\>	Mm

evaluation' in the present study, may not have been perceived as such by the hearers. The framework developed here therefore has to be seen as provisional, as is the case with any post-event description of language in context.

5.3 Text-types and goal-types

The relationship between text-types and goal-types has been outlined in the last chapter in relation to the CANCODE corpus categories. The main goal-types according to which the corpus has been classified are: collaborative idea, collaborative task and information provision. In the classification of CANCODE data, these goal-types have been used mainly to describe the structure of the text, i.e., whether the majority of the transcribed conversation is marked by a unidirectional turn structure (information-provision), or whether the transcript follows a bi-directional structure (collaborative idea/task). As already discussed, this type of classification, which is based on textual structures, cannot account for the regular occurrence of genre embedding.

In this chapter corpus data will be used to explore further an approach to the description of a speech act episode which in turn will be discussed in terms of its role in capturing goal-orientation in an unfolding conversation. This approach is opposed to the traditional description of text-types, which are applied to entire conversations (see for example Longacre 1976).

Studying suggestion episodes in a corpus can thus provide further evidence for the relationship between speaker goals and discourse structure. Episodes may be intended to solve a problem or to further the conversation. The discourse structure can be a good guide in helping to determine the goal-orientation of the speakers in this context. DeCapua and Huber (1995) point out that '[a]dvice serves to establish or maintain rapport, to flatter, to help, to reprimand, distance and dominate' (1995:128). These goal types operate at a level that mirrors speaker intention and a corpus can provide evidence for how the different goal types affect discourse structure.

5.4 Identifying a speech act episode

The *episode* has been used as a concept that is somewhat wider than the traditional units of description used particularly by proponents of the Birmingham School of Discourse Analysis, and in Conversation Analysis. Levinson (1992) uses the term *social episodes* to refer to 'activity types', which are similar to incidents of genre-oriented activity. Van Dijk (1982), on the other hand, explains 'episodes' in terms of semantic macrostructures.

The description which comes closest to the unit of analysis proposed here has been advanced by Bardovi-Harlig and Hartford (1990:481). They describe a suggestion episode as a 'sequence of turns in which a suggestion is negotiated'. They concentrate on the act directly preceding the suggestion and on the responding act to the suggestion, and they also consider a number of extended stretches of discourse. However, their data are taken from a well structured genre – the academic advising session. In casual conversation, the need expressed that triggers the suggestion may lie further back in the conversation than a single turn, as is the case in the following extract.

In this extract there are a number of evaluations starting in line 9 which eventually prompt the suggestion by speaker 4 in line 35. The episode is developed collaboratively over a number of turns by the participants in the conversation. An *episode*, as discussed in this chapter, thus refers to the negotiation of a particular

Line		
1	<S02>	Well yeah. Em look at our house. <$E> laughter <\$E>
2	<S01>	Well yes quite well yeah <$=> you <\$=> you haven't got the ability to move out
3		for a while
4	<S02>	<$G?> no spare rooms.
5	<S03>	<$E> laughs <\$E> <$G3>
6	<S01>	Yeah quite. Well no quite.
7	<S04>	Moving us out is no problem it's the stuff that er <$G?> with us.
8	<S01>	<$=> It's the <\$=> it's all the stuff yes.
9	<S04>	<$=> But er <\$=>
10	<S01>	It's not that easy. But the thing is I don't think we'd need to completely gut the
11		room any way to do it. You wouldn't tend to gut the room probably leave the bed
12		and the wardrobes in.
13	<S04>	<$G?> Well they're going to have to come out to put the hall carpet in.
14	<S01>	Yeah I suppose so. Yes. S= well yes but then that only comes out for a day doesn't
15		it.
16	<S04>	True.
17	<S01>	So you just stack the stuff everywhere while you do that.
18	<S04>	Are you going to do it yourself or are you going to get somebody <$G?>?
19	<S01>	Oh what the carpet?
20	<S04>	Yeah.
21	<S01>	Oh that'll be done.
22	<S02>	Is it square? Mhm.
23	<S01>	Oh yeah because it's got to be put down s= the gripper rail's got to go down.<$=>
24		The underlay's got to go <\$=> No I think it's worth doing it.
25	<S03>	Mm.
26	<S01>	<$=> If you're going to have reasonable carpet <\$=>
27	<S04>	Why? Then what are we all worrying about?
28	<S02>	Mhm.
29	<S03>	<$=> Th= <\$=> they'll do all the moving.
30	<S02>	Mm.
31	<S04>	<$=> The they <\$=> No what I'm thinking is what are we worrying about if
32		we're going to have him in to do that and I take it you're going to have Bob in to
33		do it?
34	<S01>	I presume so yes.
35	<S04>	Em **why don't we have him relay the hall carpet after you've had it up.**
36	<S01>	We could do yes. Yeah.

discourse function. Since episodes are constructed around a particular speech act, it is difficult to draw up general identification criteria for them. Those aspects that are studied in relation to a particular speech act episode define the length and nature of the episode. In this chapter, the main focus of the suggestion episode is on *agency* and *time frame* of the suggestion, as these were identified as relevant criteria for the functional profile of speech act expressions in previous chapters.

Agency, as will be further discussed below, is expressed through the relationship between the speaker who elicits a suggestion, or gives information that is addressed by the suggestion, and the participant who makes the suggestion. Furthermore, the notion of agency needs to account for the person who is named as the agent in the suggestion and his/her role vis-a-vis the other discourse participants. The episode begins at the point when one of the participants makes a statement that is addressed by the suggestion. Any preceeding negative evaluations that are part of the general topic but not directly addressed by the suggestion are here not seen as part of the episode. The same applies to responses that occur subsequent to the 'first response' following the suggestion. For analytical purposes, it is important that the episode unit is kept relatively small. A larger unit would be prone to interference of aspects of other speech acts that are better studied as part of separate speech act episodes.

5.4.1 Agency in suggestion episodes

Agency in suggestion episodes has traditionally been described in terms of the 'commitment' on the part of the hearer, and has therefore focused on the person who is supposed to carry out the proposed line of action introduced by the suggestion (Brown & Levinson 1987; Tsui 1994; Longacre 1983). Suggestions can imply that an action will be carried out by the hearer, the speaker and hearer, or just the speaker. This very narrow description is based on previous research on suggestions which has primarily focused on the speaker and hearer as agents. Marmaridou (1988) offers a definition of suggestions as

> a language function whereby one of the interlocutors may express his/her belief that a course of action is possible and desirable for him/herself and/or the addressee, and that this course of action could be profitably taken up by either or both of them, as the case may be (1988: 126).

In the corpus data, on the other hand, there are plenty of examples in which suggestions are not only concerned with the actions of the speaker or hearer, but include other people or organisations as the extract below shows:

<S01><$=> And then the sort of question related to all that is **why not use erm** </$=>. If if if you have to repeat the exercise in other studies you can't can't this one figure's valid elsewhere. **Why not use a multi-centred approach up front**. This may be more costly in the short term but then you know you get a cross section of all intensive care units and er er y= you don't just base it on the one teaching hospital. I'd just like to sort of <$G?> people on on that. Okay. So maybe a multi-site er multi-site multi-study application. A question there. A question of when when will average costs suffice. Just an average cost per patient or per patient day. Well it's obvious that when there's a big resources variation tha=

tha= tha= tha= tha= that's when you you need it and maybe intensive care is is is obviously and important candidate for that. But also is it every study that includes intensive or only those studies where intensive care is the major part of the total cost of of of of the er the treatment or the intervention. So it's almost where the dividing line where you you want to measure out in in reality or you want to use the approximation. Er otherwise well well if it.

This extract is taken from a professional discussion between health economists. During an extended speaker turn, speaker 1 presents an argument for a 'multi-centred approach' to intensive care. His suggestion *why not use a multi-centered approach* does not refer to the actions of anyone in the conversation but to an organisation (the National Health Service) in general. Neither is the suggestion elicited by any of the other speakers. Instead, speaker 1 identifies the need for the suggestion himself: 'you get a cross section of all intensive care units'. The interpretation of agency in terms of speaker or hearer commitment expressed in the proposition is thus too narrow as a concept to account for the suggestion episodes discussed here. A description of the process is needed which takes into account the person who solicits the suggestion, the person who makes a suggestion and the person named as an agent in the proposition.

5.4.1.1 *Inclusive and exclusive agency*
The speech act expressions that might offer an interesting starting point for comparison are those that are semantically different in terms of the type of agency, for example, inclusive, exclusive and 'others as agents'. It is thus useful to return to those expressions discussed in Chapter 4: *why don't we*, *why don't you* and *why not*.

The use of *why don't we* in the extract above, for example, shows this expression being used in a way that makes agency opaque. This is not unexpected since the focus of the extract is on deciding on certain procedures, rather than on who is to carry out those procedures. It resembles what Longacre (1983) has called 'procedural discourse' where the emphasis is on *how to do it* rather than *who does it*. The discussion in this chapter thus included delineation of the factors that determine the agency status introduced by speech act expressions.

There are two main types of suggestions in which the addressee of the suggestion does not tend to be part of the conversation: *reported suggestions*, and *direct suggestions* that refer to people other than the ones present in the conversation. The next extract is an example of the former.

Examples in the corpus where reported suggestions are introduced by *why don't you* are easily found, especially in the *socio-cultural* and *intimate* category. These two context categories are also the ones in which we would expect to find most 'gossip' episodes (see Eggins & Slade 1997 for a discussion). Reported suggestions tend to be exclusive in terms of agency, but can also be inclusive when, for

Line		
1	\<S01\>	Cos like he came out with me and I didn't really persuade him. He said he'd come
2		anyway but+
3	\<S03\>	Mm.
4	\<S01\>	+I knew I could've persuaded him. And and I thought we had quite a nice day.
5		And we got back in and he seemed okay. Erm and I was just talking quite a lot
6		about "You have to learn to trust people" and all this stuff about not inflicting
7		himself. And I said **"Why don't you stay for tea?"** and he said "Oh I've inflicted
8		myself enough on you already." I said "Benny you've been helping me with the
9		work."
10	\<S03\>	Mm.

example, an event is being told in which the speaker him or herself was involved. As argued earlier, suggestions in which the proposed action refers to people other than the ones present in the conversation, are often related to 'making a point' or 'criticising'. They tend to follow a different goal-sub-type to the ones where the agents are participants in the conversation.

5.4.1.2 *Solicited* versus *unsolicited advice*

DeCapua and Huber (1995), in a discussion of advice in American English, distinguish between *solicited* and *unsolicited* advice on the following grounds:

> In unsolicited advice, the advice-givers take upon themselves the role of expert, authority and concerned person. In solicited advice, advice seekers explicitly request the help of another person whom they believe has both expertise and concern for their problems.   (DeCapua & Huber 1995: 122)

They use questionnaires to elicit information about whom subjects would consult for advice. A number of 'advice-givers' are identified, such as mother, parents, brother, and others. These tended to be prefered choices for informants, usually because of their credentials ('Mom. She always knows what to do') (1995: 125). The questionnaire itself states a number of potential problem situations. One of the scenarios is: 'If you were going to adopt a dog, which people and/or sources would you turn to for help?', and another 'You and your girl/boyfriend just no longer seem to be getting along, no matter what you do. Which people and/or sources would you turn to for help?' (DeCapua & Huber 1995: 129).

Since no real interactional data is used in this study, it is difficult to assess how the informants would go about soliciting the kind of advice discussed in the questionnaire. The extracts in this chapter illustrate that the value of questionnaires to assess the process of soliciting advice may be methodologically questionable. Although the authors maintain that 'Our questionnaire responses and observations suggest that in the course of daily conversation, advice-giving, receiving, and requesting occurs frequently, often informally, and unremarkably' (1995: 124), the kinds of questions asked suggest a clear intention on the advisee's part. While De-Capua & Huber set out to describe scenarios that may take place in daily conversation, the CANCODE data suggest that in everyday language-in-use, advice-giving episodes are often constructed collaboratively, emerging from the participants' contributions to the conversation, rather than being based on a predetermined intention to seek advice. Often a particular topic 'triggers' an episode, as one of the speakers expresses a concern or negative evaluation. The extract below illustrates this observation:

Line			Comments
1	<S01>	Wasn't there some trouble in the village yesterday?	
2		Haven't I missed something? A car went out of control or some-	
3		thing?	
4	<$?F>	Who?	
5	<S01>	<$=> Wendy went i= </$=> I don't know. My daughter Wendy	**Gossip I**
6		went+	
7	<$?F>	<$G?>	
8	<S01>	+into the Post Office and they were all discussing it.	
9	<S03>	<$G?>	
10	<S01>	A car had gone out of control I think.	
11	<$?F>	<$G?>	
12	<$?F>	<$G?> don't they.	
13	<$?F>	No.	
14	<S01>	<$E> tuts </$E> Oh well.	
15	<S02>	Er anyway I'd better get back. <$E> laughs </$E>	
16	<S03>	It'll probably be this man+	
17	<$?F>	<$G?>	
18	<S03>	+he was parked <$=> in bar= er </$=> outside Barclays Bank.	
19			
20			
21	<S02>	Anyway see you later.	End of
22	<S01>	Bye Wendy.	previous
23	<S03>	Bye.	service
24	<S02>	Ta ta.	encounter
25			
26	<S03>	And left <$X> t' \| the </$X> car running and locked the keys in	
27		<$X> t' \| the </$X> car as well.	
28	<S01>	S=s=someone had what?	**Gossip I** contd.
29	<$?F>	<$H> Had gone. </$H>	
30			
31	<$?M>	Got no cigarettes?	
32	<S03>	No. Sorry we haven't love.	New service
33	<$?M>	Oh.	encounter
34	<S03>	Post Office.	
35	<S01>	He'd what?	

36	<S03>	Gone into Barclays Bank. Well gone to <$X> t' \| the </$X> thing	
37		you know.	
38	<S01>	Yes.	**Gossip I contd.**
39	<S03>	And locked his car door with <$X> t' \| the </$X> keys in and car	
40		bloody running and all.	
41	<S01>	Oh dear.	
42	<$E>	laughs </$E>	
43	<S01>	So what happened there?	
44	<S03>	I don't know Mags. <$G?> When I first came in this morning	
45		<$G?>.	
46	<S01>	I'm a bit deaf again Marie. <$=> I'll have to go and have my ears	
47		do= </$=> I think it's swimming you know.	
48			
49	<S03>	Oh it is. **Why don't you get some plugs for your ears?** <$E> uses	**Suggestion**
50		till </$E> <$G?> **Just put it in before you go.**	**Episode**
51			
52	<S01>	<$=> I might I </$=> I might have to do that.	
53	<$?M>	<$G?>	
54	<S01>	<$=> If it </$=>	
55	<S03>	See I got some from <$X> t' \| the </$X> doctors once	
56		even for washing my hair. Because I kept getting this	
57		ear infection. Ear infection. You mustn't get any water	
58		in it. He said Don't go swimming or anything. And	
59		then er he said Give you some plugs he says and	
60		when you wash your hair put these plugs in.	
61	<S01>	And did it help?	
62	<S03>	Oh aye. I use them all <$X> t' \| the </$X> time.	
63	<S01>	Oh you do it now even.	
64	<S03>	And I got some from Boots's chemist in town.	
65	<S01>	Oh right.	
66	<S03>	<$G?>	
67	<S01>	<$=> I might </$=> I might have to look out for	
68		something+	
69	<S03>	Mm.	
70	<S01>	+like that.	
71	<S03>	Yeah.	
72	<S01>	Cos it+	
73	<S03>	<$=> Well I </$=>	
74	<S01>	+is a problem.	
75	<S03>	Yes. Aye. And this woman come after you'd been in	
76		<$G?> Are you lip-reading?	
77	<S01>	N=no. I can't really.	
78	<$E>	laughs </$E>	
79	<S01>	I'm not a good lip reader.	

This extract is taken from a conversation between a customer and a shop assistant in a news agent's. The two speakers know each other well. They are friends who talk about general events in the village. Eggins and Slade (1997:278) define this kind of interaction as 'talk which involves pejorative judgement of an absent other'. In this extract, speaker 1 elicits a gossip episode with a question about an incident that happened in the village. Speaker 3 volunteers information about the event in question. Pejorative judgement occurs in a number of places, and is realised lexically by terms such as *out of control* and *car bloody running and all* (lines 2–3, 10, 40). The gossip episodes are interrupted by complete (Interruption 2) and incomplete (Interruption 1) service encounters, which yet again exemplifies the dynamic nature of generic activity.

In this extract it seems that the episode is triggered because speaker 1 has problems in understanding what speaker 3 is saying and expresses this by stating *I'm a bit deaf again Marie*. As such, she makes a negative evaluation about her own hearing and offers a possible reason for this problem (swimming). Speaker 3, in turn, offers a suggestion – *to use earplugs* – which she reinforces by telling a story which involved herself facing a similar problem. DeCapua and Huber (1995:125) observe similar strategies for solicited advice in their data, which they see as an 'attempt to maintain equal status, thereby avoiding unwarranted bossiness'. There is a further de-focalisation of agency in the suggestion offered by speaker 3. Lines 53–79 do not form part of the episode in the model of description suggested here, as the proposed model only includes the 'first response'. However, a strong case could be made for an 'extended episode' as an analytical unit which could include topical progression that follows on from the speech act that forms the 'core' of the episode. The study of extended episodes may lead to the identification of a number of further strategies preceding and following the speech act – an issue which has only been dealt with marginally in the present study. However, in order to establish the 'extended episode' as a unit, we need to first understand the variations within the 'core' which is the focus of this chapter.

Interestingly, the episode above would not count as 'solicited advice' in DeCapua and Huber's definition, since there is no act of ostensible advice seeking. There is a difference, according to the authors, between unsolicited advice issued by strangers and that issued by friends. While the latter is usually accepted as part of the socialising process, the former is often cause for offence.

Hoey (1983) argues that a problem in discourse will generally be expressed in terms of 'negative evaluation + need'. This description seems to be a useful starting point for delineating the episode, as it allows a distinction to be made between *unsolicited versus solicited* advice. A close investigation of the discourse immediately preceding the suggestion or advice can then help place the speech act on a scale ranging from advice that is sought explicitly to situations in which the need or negative evaluation is not made explicit. In-between these two polar opposites, there are situations in which a direct need or negative evaluation are expressed either explicitly, or where it is implicit in the context.

This model then serves as the basic structural framework for the description of 'pre-suggestion' utterances. The notions of need and need perception are further discussed in the next section.

5.5 Pattern of problem solving

In the speech act episodes in the CANCODE corpus which were studied for the purpose of developing a structural model, there are two reasons why a 'need state-ment' may be absent from an episode. The first one is because the need is implicit in the direct context, as in the example below:

Line		
1	<S02>	But+
2	<S01>	An evaporating dish is quite good.
3	<S02>	+<$=> but <$G3> wouldn't it </$=> wouldn't it say burn if er you wanted it to
4		burn? <$E> *sniffs* </$E>
5	<S01>	Well yeah. I'd have thought so. **Why don't you get yourself a tissue?** <$=> The
6		erm </$=> An evaporating dish is a good idea. Something that's even better is
7		called a erm+ <$E> *blows nose* </$E>
8	<S01>	+crucible.
9	<S02>	Well we haven't used them.

In this extract, the suggestion refers to an imminent need for the suggestion (speaker 2 sniffs). The suggestion *Why don't you get yourself a tissue* does not follow a negative evaluation or a need statement and could thus be regarded as 'unsolicited'. However, since it is related to an immediate need perception located within the situation (sniffing), it follows a somewhat different purpose than the suggestions discussed above. There are a number of other suggestions in the cor-pus in which the need arises from the immediate context, usually when people are engaged in a task. The lack of video records of the transcribed interactions make this kind of structure particularly difficult to assess in mono-modal corpora. The analyst must here rely on contextual information added during the transcription process.

The second reason why a need statement may be absent is that the suggestion is not geared towards a 'problem' in Hoey's (1983) sense. Consider the next extract which is taken from a conversation between family members.

Line		
1	<S02>	<$E> speaks with mouth full </$E> That's what he's on about. He's on about
2		buying a house in Ireland and <$=> using it </$=> having it as a boarding house.
3	<S01>	Bed and breakfast.
4	<S02>	Weren't you.
5	<S01>	Yeah.
6	<S02>	Bed and breakfast as well.
7	<S01>	Mm.
8	<S03>	**Why don't you have it in the Lake District and I'll come and help you.** <$E>
9		laughs </$E>
10	<S01>	Well you can come to Ireland with us.

Here the 'focus' of the suggestion episode shifts in terms of the 'time dimension' in which the suggested action is supposed to take place. What is addressed is not a 'problem' but a future situation that has no anchor in the past. The goal-type changes with this shift in time dimension from 'problem-solving' to 'reaching agreement about future plans'.

The discussion above has illustrated a number of important issues regarding the nature of the suggestion episode, as well as the relationship between various descriptive components within the episode and the emerging goal-types. It is important to note that while the different stages of solicited versus unsolicited advice are often directly related to the goal-type, they are not dependent on it. They therefore form a useful descriptive apparatus for suggestion episodes in different situations. The discussion so far has illustrated the following points:

- In order to integrate goal-orientation into the discourse analysis framework, the unit of description for suggestion episodes needs to include the notion of agency. Agency can be described in terms of the dynamic turn options within the episode;
- In order to describe the dialogic nature of agency, the suggestion episode needs to start with the utterance that is addressed by the suggestion;
- The type of utterance that is addressed by the suggestion can be either a negative evaluation, a need statement, or simply a piece of information.
- This more fine-grained distinction does not only contribute to the interpretation of goal-types, but also highlights the fact that in the corpus data suggestions are hardly ever unsolicited.

The following section will further describe the notion of need perception used in the cline of solicited and unsolicited advice above.

5.5.1 Suggestions and time reference

One of the salient features of need perception is the time frame of the suggestion. The 'time frame' which is attached to a certain action not only impacts on the rate of the imposition (Brown & Levinson 1987), but also interacts with the goal of the suggestion. Hasan (1999) argues that

> 'there is thus a cline of goal awareness, the two endpoints of which have been re-ferred to as visible and invisible goal, respectively. Visible goals tend to be short term: they are achieved (or not) typically within one interaction; by contrast invisible goals tend to be long term [...]' (1999: 234).

There are two aspects of the 'time dimension' which are important in this context. One is related to the 'need' as expressed by one of the participants, and the other to the time frame of the suggested action. Brown and Levinson (1987) argue that the more urgent the need, the more baldly we express a proposition. This implies that we are less likely to find solicited advice when the need is urgent. The time frame in which the suggested action is to be completed is therefore an important part of the episode but as yet, there is little corpus-based research into the effects of different time-frames on discourse structure.

Longacre (1983) discusses the issue of 'completion' of a suggested event in procedural discourse. *Procedural discourse*, a genre category traditionally applied to written monologue (Martin 1989), encapsulates a main aim of prescribing, of telling someone 'how to do something', and the individual steps involved in this process. The distinction between the 'time frame' of the need and the 'time frame' of the action is important as it suggests differences in goal-types. Thus, in suggestion episodes where there is no need statement, and the time frame for the action is either immediate or in the future, the goal-type is more likely to be one of 'planning' or 'developing ideas or activities' rather than 'problem-solving' or 'advice-giving'. The only exception to this is when the need is explicit through the immediate context, in which case the goal type is likely to be 'problem-solving'.

The following extracts illustrate this point. The first extract shows how speakers develop an idea or a plan that lies in the future, while the second extract is concerned with solving a problem that has its anchor in the past.

Line		
1	<S02>	What next door did when they found some glass in their soup they sent it off and
2		they had loads of soup sent to them.
3	<S01>	I'm going to send it off but listen **why don't we just find pieces of plastic in the**
4		**house** <$E> laughs </$E> **and just write to them and** <$=> **say that we** </$=>
5		<$E> laughter </$E>.
6	<S02>	Shall we not eh? Shall we just get done for say that we found it and then they'll
7		send us load of soups fraud. Oh I found this television in this can of soup.

8	<S01>	<$=> Yeah but if we get </$=> <$=> Er well </$=> <$E> laughs </$E>
9	<S02>	Well I found this spatula in this can of soup and I must say <$O17> <$=> I'm s=
10		</$=> <$E> pause </$E>+
11	<S01>	<$E> coughs </$E>
12	<S02>	+I'm so disgusted at your
13	<S01>	You can do it with chocolate as well with Maltesers they bring you a massive box
14		of them. So if we just get a Malteser and make it deformed and like make it all
15		weird inside.
16	<S02>	Like by eating it

The next extract is an example of a speech act episode in which the suggestion refers to an explicitly expressed need, and where the goal-type is more likely to be one of problem-solving:

Line		
1	<S01>	Aye bloody <$E> pause <\$E> keeps going picture keeps going blue like just going
2		blue.
3	<S02>	Oh our picture doesn't go blue <$G?> black and white telly.
4	<$E>	laughs <\$E>
5	<S01>	<$G?> could well be. It hasn't got no colour now either it just comes on <$G?>
6		comes on black and white <$G?>
7	<S02>	Well <$G?> just turn <$G?> just turn your colour off. If you turn your colour
8		right off if you watched in black and white.
9	<S01>	I know. Well
10	<S02>	But I mean <$=> that <\$=> that's nothing <$G?> in blue.
11	<S03>	It isn't not when you pay eighty odd pound on colour licence.
12	<S02>	**Why don't you tell them to come and mend it then.**
13	<S03>	Well it shouldn't break down.
14	<S01>	<$O93> Oh no nowadays.
15	<S02>	You know.

In this extract, the turns leading up to the suggestion articulate a problem. The time frame for the suggested line of action is projected, while the time-frame of the need is anchored in the past. Since the speaker who initiates the suggestion episode by expressing a problem is different to the participant who puts forward the suggestion in line 12, the goal-type of 'problem-solving' is linked to a text-type of 'advice giving'.

5.6 Categorising replies

So far the turns and sequential options preceding a suggestion as well as elements that are addressed by the suggestion have been discussed. This section deals with the reply options to a suggestion. These form the final element in the episode. The reply that follows an initiating act can reveal a great deal about how the act has been understood by the hearer, yet responses have not received much attention in the speech act literature, which has mainly focussed on initiating acts (Austin 1962; Fraser 1975; Bach & Harnish 1979; Searle 1976).

Reply options are incorporated into the wider framework of describing the suggestion episode. Replies have been studied extensively in relation to 'advice' by conversation analysts (Heritage & Sefi 1992; Jefferson & Lee 1992), especially with a view to understanding how people 'reject' advice in institutional settings. However, in casual conversation suggestions are more varied and replies are less predictable.

Tsui (1994) devises a taxonomy of replies which takes into account the function of the initiating act. She differentiates between 'responses' and 'challenges'. Her assessment of moves is based on illocutionary intent and pragmatic presuppositions of the initiating move. Hence, if the intent of a question is to receive information, a response that provides information is seen as a 'positive responding act' (1994: 165). An utterance that does not provide this information, on the other hand, is seen as a challenge. The four initiating acts can yield the following moves:

Elicit: response	–	elicit: challenge
Request: response	–	request: challenge
Direct: response	–	direct: challenge
Inform: response	–	inform: challenge

Tsui's framework is based on the division into *moves* and *acts* proposed by Sinclair and Coulthard (1975). Burton (1981) also draws on the Sinclair and Coulthard model (1975), and argues that it may not be suitable in the study of conversations outside the classroom as it does not account for a variety of moves which we can expect to find in everyday conversation. Burton (1981) lists seven types of move: *framing, focussing, opening, supporting, challenging, bound-opening* and *re-opening*. The division into *supporting* and *challenging* moves accounts better for the collaborative and dynamic character of everyday interaction than the framework proposed by Sinclair and Coulthard (1975). This aspects is thus important for the description of the interactional character of the suggestion episodes in CANCODE.

5.6.1 Supporting moves

Burton (1980) explains supporting moves in terms of Halliday's (1978) functions of language: *ideational+textual* and *interpersonal*. The first two aspects (*ideational+textual*) are defined lexico-sematically within the topic-component, and are analysed in terms of Halliday and Hasan's (1976) concept of *cohesion*.

This means that a supporting move needs to display cohesion with the preceding move. The interpersonal aspect is explained in terms of interdependant and reciprocal acts and the expected second-pair parts to an initiatory act. Examples of act-combinations for supporting moves in this framework are:

Marker – acknowledge
Summons – accept
Metastatement – accept
Informative – acknowledge
Elicitation – reply
Directive – react
Accuse – excuse

By using both the *ideational* and the *interpersonal* aspect, the descriptive framework requires a reply to support either the topic or the speaker for a move to be classified as supporting. The following extract illustrates the difference between *supporting topic* and *supporting speaker* turns:

Line		
1	<S02>	Well they've been back here once+
2	<$?M>	<$H> Boof. </$H> <$E> laughs </$E>
3	<S02>	+or twice. And the police said We can't do nothing.
4	<S03>	No.
5	<S01>	Mm.
6	<S03>	<$=> It's against the </$=>
7	<S02>	Because they've gone again. Well+
8	<S03>	They'll be back.
9	<S02>	+in perhaps about another two or three weeks they'll be back again.
10	<S03>	They'll be back again.
11	<S02>	Now what everybody suggested to the police is well **why not put some sort of type**
12		**of stumps all across**+
13	<S01>	Mm.
14	<S02>	+the edge of of it+
15	<S03>	Yes. Yeah.
16	<S01>	So they can't drive their vehicles+
17	<S03>	Mm.

In this extract speaker 1 is supporting the move by speaker 2, in an informative-acknowledge sequence. However, in the last but one turn speaker 1 supports the topic. The extract shows convergence between the speakers and, according to Burton, is doubly supportive. The hearer has no reason to disagree with the speaker since the speaker is not addressing him directly with his suggestion.

However, this framework is not without problems. It is, for example, not clear whether a *backchannel* should count as an *acknowledging* move, which would make it a supporting move in terms of the 'reciprocal act' framework. 'Acknowledging' replies must be seen as the main reciprocal act for a suggestion, since a suggestion has been identified as 'putting forward an idea for consideration' to which the expected reply would be an 'acknowledge'. Acceptance can be signalled through the use of *backchannels* but also by *laughter*, or by 'sentence completion' (Duncan 1972).

There is a key difference in those instances where acceptance is signalled by physical action. The following request, for example, has been accepted by way of compliance, showing that acceptance can be signalled verbally, as well as physically depending on the type of suggestion or request:

> D: Leave me matches alone! I'm telling you a joke.
> C: Right, what's that.
> (from Tsui 1994: 178)

Before considering the use of challenging moves, the issue of accepting a suggestion requires further discussion. It has been argued above that backchannels should be considered as an 'acknowledging move', but it is not clear whether backchannel replies should count as supporting moves or not. Yngve (1970) introduces the term as a type of minimal response which signals to the speaker that the hearer is still paying attention (see also Schegloff 1982). However, the notion of 'attention' does not necessarily coincide with the notion of 'understanding'. It seems then that minimal responses, such as 'mmh' and 'uhuh' cannot be counted as 'supporting moves' as such, but rather need to be considered in terms of their discourse function of signalling attention. Eggins and Slade (1997: 204) use the term 'registering moves' which 'provide supportive encouragement for the other speaker to take another turn'. This view shifts the focus from 'supporting the speaker or the topic' to 'accepting the information of the prior move as well as the discourse role of the participant'. This approach seems to be more appropriate in the context of the framework developed here. The moves that count as supporting moves are thus those which support explicitly either the topic or the speaker, while 'backchannel' items are seen as 'accepting' information that is being given, rather than supporting it. This means that there is a cline which reaches from 'supporting moves' to 'accept', to 'challenge' of a suggestion.

5.6.2 Challenging moves

Eggins and Slade (1997: 206) argue that '[c]onfronting responses can range from either disengaging (refusing to participate in the exchange, for example, by responding with silence), or by offering a confronting reply'. 'Conflictual' or 'challenging moves', according to Burton (1981), 'hold up the progress of [that] topic or topic-introduction in some way' (1981: 71), as in the example following:

Line
1 `<S01>` `<$O43>` `<$G?>` I would suggest `</$O43>` that we take your bag inside then
2   `<$O44>` you'll feel happier `</$O44>`.
3 `<S02>` `<$O44>` But that's what I said. `</$O44>`

The response line 3 *But that's what I said* does not comply with the pattern of reciprocal acts, and hence challenges the initiatory move. This is also a useful example to illustrate the difference between challenging a speaker and challenging a topic. Here, speaker 2 challenges the speaker while supporting the topic.

Presuppositions as discussed by Searle (1969) can be useful in the classification of challenges to suggestions. Tsui (1994:178) lists the following presuppositions for *advisives*:

a. 'the speaker believes that there is a need for the advocated action;
b. the speaker believes that the advocated action is in the interest of the addressee;
c. the addressee is able and willing to carry out the action;
d. it is not obvious that the addressee will carry out the action of his/her own accord'.

The reply by speaker 2 in the last extract challenges the last of these presuppositions in that the speaker expresses that she would have taken the bags inside anyway. The notion of 'challenging topic' versus 'challenging speaker' would relate to (c) and (d) as a *speaker challenge*, while challenges to the others implies a *topic challenge*.

However, the presuppositions above only take into account those suggestions in which the hearer is the addressee of the suggestion. Presupposition (b) therefore needs to be amended slightly for the purpose of analysing the examples from the CANCODE corpus and incorporate suggestions with 'others as agents':

b. the speaker believes that the advocated action is in the interest of the agent named in the suggestion or the beneficiary of the suggestion if different from the agent and
c. the addressee or agent implied in the suggestion is able (and willing) to carry out the action.

This reformulation allows for 'assessments' to be taken into account, as the following example illustrates.

In this episode, speaker 1 makes an assessment, which Tsui (1994:183) identifies as 'the speaker's judgement or evaluation of people, object(s), events, or state(s) of affairs'. The reply by speaker 3 would be classified in the current analysis as a challenge with respect to presupposition (b). The preferred reply would have been an 'accept' of speaker 1's evaluation.

Line		
1	<S01>	You know and I mean <$=> it </$=> you know **why not sort of make it a bit**
2		**more reasonable you know the the first prize** you know have a limit of of say I
3		dunno you know a couple of million which is enough anyway for God's sake.
4	<S03>	But they wouldn't be better off this week you know half the money or or whoever
5		wins it you know to to try and do something for these+

5.6.3 Clarifying moves

One further type of response that has not yet been discussed is that of 'requesting clarification'. Eggins and Slade (1997:210) see moves that 'seek additional information in order to understand a prior move' as types of supporting moves 'in the sense that they merely delay anticipated exchange completion' (1997:207). On the cline between supporting and challenging moves, they tend towards the challenging end, since they 'hold up the discourse' (Burton 1980), and restructure the exchange complex. The following is an example of a clarifying move:

Line		
1	<S02>	<$G2> and me we was talking about it in the summer. **Hey why don't we just s=**
		do a swap.
2	<S04>	<$H> With the </$H> family?

Here, speaker 4 asks for clarification of the suggestion put forward by speaker 2. He seeks further information about the proposed action before he can commit to an answer.

5.6.4 Detaching moves

Instances in which there is no verbal response to a suggestion, but which are instead marked by 'compliance' have already been discussed. 'Compliance' is realised by carrying out the action named in the suggestion. The absence of a verbal response in 'compliance' needs to be distinguished from a deliberate ignoring move, as well as from the absence of a verbal response where one would have been expected. Eggins and Slade (1997:211) discuss 'detaching moves' which 'seek to terminate the interaction'. Detaching moves can be realised either by 'silence' or 'expression of termination' (1997:213). The notion of detaching moves is useful and will be integrated into the current model. However, apart from the two realisations mentioned by Eggins and Slade, 'topic change' will also be counted as a detaching move. This is illustrated in the following example.

Here speaker 3 seems to 'ignore' the suggestion put forward by speaker 2, and shifts the topic from 'the gift' to 'the looks of the daughter'. While the two are

Line		
1	\<S03\>	He usually comes with a bottle of wine.
2	\<S01\>	On Christmas Eve?
3	\<S03\>	Yes. And I never have anything for him.
4	\<S01\>	Uh huh.
5	\<S03\>	So I'd better have a box of sweets for the children.
6	\<S02\>	God. \<$E\> laughs \</$E\> You're not giving those expensive ones.
7	\<S03\>	No. No.
8	\<S02\>	Well **why not give him a bottle of something?**
9	\<S03\>	His eldest daughter \<$H\> Nora \</$H\> is the most beautiful looking girl.
10	\<S01\>	Is she?
11	\<S03\>	You'd stop in the street. \<$G1\> you know. \<$H\> And even so you know \</$H\>
12		she's so nice.

related, the suggestion remains unattended to. Detaching moves cannot easily be described in terms of supporting or challenging properties since they are related to different aspects of the interaction. They say more about the structure of the discourse than about the attitude towards the suggestion. They therefore have to be treated as a separate category.

5.7 Reporting problems and reported suggestions

One of the issues of many structural models of Discourse Analysis is that they are not easily applied to monologues. This, of course, poses a problem for an account of suggestions in a corpus where many suggestions are reported and occur in a narrative sequence.

While reported suggestions can still be analysed in the broad terms of the framework outlined above, adjustments have to be made with regard to the speaker options within the episode. Thus, in reported suggestions, the speaker who expresses the need or problem is often identical with the speaker who offers the suggestion. Hence, a somewhat different framework is required to assess reported suggestions. The question of agency remains important and should be reflected in the framework. Reported suggestions in the corpus occur in the form of speech reporting as well as thought reporting (see Leech & Short 1981). The choice of speech act expression obviously restricts the narrating tenses. The speech act expressions analysed for the purpose of this chapter can only be reported through direct speech. However, this may not merely be a reflection of the types of expressions chosen for this study. In his study of CANCODE data, McCarthy (1998: 161) finds that '[...] in the narrative texts in the CANCODE corpus, speech reports are overwhelmingly direct speech, and with reporting verbs in past simple (said, told) or historical present says'. One of the reasons for this is to add to the 'vividness' and 'real-time staging' (ibid) of the discourse. Furthermore, replicating direct speech adds to the authenticity of a narrative.

Line		
1	<S02>	So what happened? Did you come into the house then? Was Sue there?
2	<S03>	No.
3	<S05>	Stood at stood at <$X> t' | the <\$X> gate.
4	<S03>	Just stood at <$X> t' | the <\$X> gate talking didn't we. And he says "**Ooh how**
5		**about coming down**" Didn't you. Well that took till September.
6	<S01>	<$E> laughs <\$E>
7	<S03>	<$G?> to go on holiday somewhere.
8	<S05>	<$G?> oh I've still got my dance partners and
10	<S05>	what have you.

In this extract, speaker 3 relates a past event that involves herself and speaker 5. The goal-type seems to be that of 'entertaining'. The story itself has what Eggins and Slade (1997: 237), following Plum (1988), call the character of an 'anecdote' which involves 'the retelling of events with a prosody of evaluation running throughout to make the story worth telling'. The evaluation in the 'recount' above is realised by the statement *Well that took till September*.

5.7.1 Integrating agency into story-telling genres

While the type of agency in reported suggestions is related to the type of story-telling genre, Plum's story-telling genres are not explicitly defined in terms of agency. However, since the notion of *agency* has been defined as a main property of the suggestion episode, it seems important to incorporate this focus into the description of narrated suggestions.

While it would be beyond the scope of this study to redefine all storytelling genres in terms of the type of agency that they exhibit, the four types of story-telling genres discussed above are here joined with Hasan's (1999) model of 'recounting' events to present the various options of 'agency' within a system network.

Hasan (1999), in her discussion of narrative as a feature of field, outlines a model to account for choices of narrating sequences which is based on 'agency', 'structure' and 'time-frame' (see Figure 5.1).

The distinction between 'personal' and 'communal' allows for an integration of the aspect of agency in that a reported suggestion episode that is marked 'personal' refers to an episode that tells an event which involved the speaker [personal:self] or another person [personal:other]. The terms *episode* and *sequence* are closely related to Plum's criteria for distinguishing 'narratives and anecdotes' from

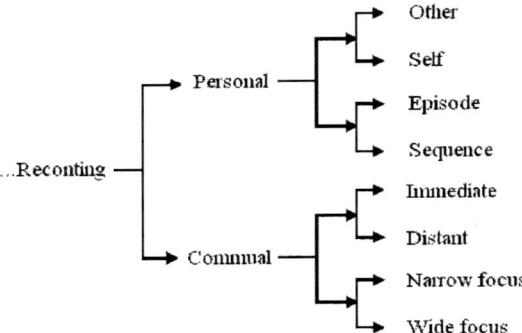

Figure 5.1 Hasan's (1999: 294) model of recounting events

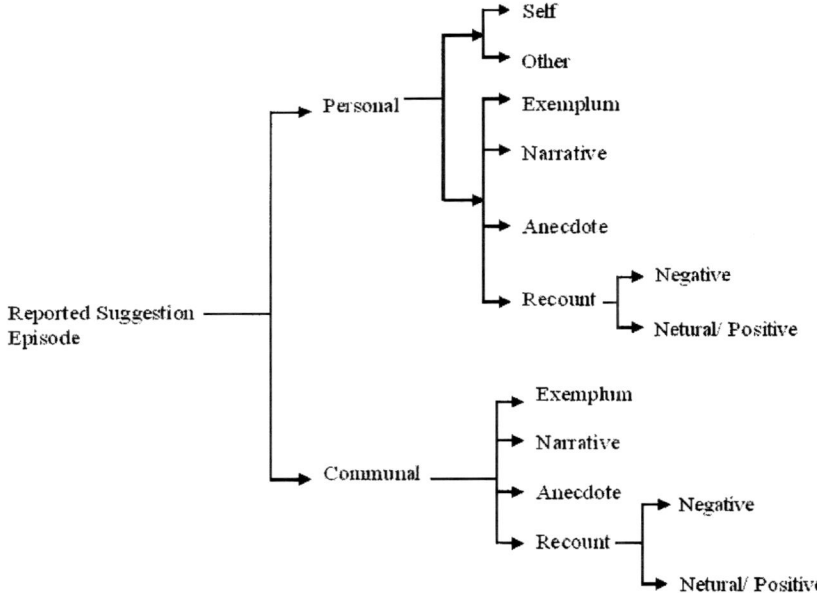

Figure 5.2 Reported suggestion episodes (based on Hasan 1999: 294, adapted and extended model)

'exemplums and recounts', in that the former is concerned with relating a particular event (episode) with the focus on the resolution or 'crisis' generated by this event, while the latter is more concerned with a sequenced account of events in order to evaluate (as in recounts) or bring out a point about the state of the world (as in exemplums). Since Plum's model incorporates the notion of *aim* more readily than Hasan's model, Hasan's 'episodes' and 'sequences' are here replaced with the four story-telling genres proposed by Plum.

'Communal' recounts, on the other hand, focus on 'a (section of the) community as a whole' (Hasan 1999: 295). Hasan's notion of 'communal:immediate' and 'communal:distant' refers to the difference in time scale, i.e., whether an event lies in the distant past (e.g. historical event) or the nearer past. The difference between *narrow focus* and *wide focus*, on the other hand, refers to whether the event described focuses on a particular 'story' or on a feature of communal significance. These two aspects are not as important for the model developed here as the events described in suggestion episodes generally lie in the near past and the focus is generally narrow. Only the various types of narrative discussed above present the options following the 'communal' choice. The choices of reported suggestions are summarised in Figure 5.2 above.

A study of the speech act expressions *why not*, *why don't you* and *why don't we* in CANCODE shows that they play an important part in the linguistic repertoire for reporting suggestions, and it is therefore paramount that a framework for analysing lexico-grammatical realisations of speech acts takes reported structures into account. It still needs to be tested whether their functional profiles, i.e., their contextual associations and the goal types in which they occur remain stable in reported structures. The framework outlined above might be a useful starting point to investigate this particular issue further.

5.8 Summary

Drawing on examples of suggestions in the CANCODE corpus which are introduced by a specific set of speech act expressions, this chapter has started to outline a possible corpus-based framework for analysing and categorising suggestion episodes. It was argued that traditional discourse models have to be extended to account for the examples found in the corpus.

It was further proposed that the suggestion episode should be viewed as a component in a wider model of context. This model takes into account the relationship between the speakers, as well as the goals of the interaction. The two main aspects discussed in this chapter are *agency* and *time-frame*, as they emerged from the suggestion episodes in the corpus. Rather than assigning agency on the basis of the semantics of the speech act expression, the model assigns commitment and benefit agents on the basis of the sequence that constitutes the episode. It has thus been possible to achieve a more empirical account of agency and authority in suggestions. The time-frame is another aspect that has often been neglected in previous studies of speech acts. Based on the corpus examples the framework developed in this chapter distinguishes between the time frame of the 'need', and the time frame of the 'proposed action', which allows for a more delicate linkage with goal-types.

As regards the status of suggestions as being either *solicited* or *unsolicited*, it was argued that we need to establish a more fine-grained definition of these seemingly polar categories in the light of the diversity of acts that precede the suggestion. The description of these acts has also contributed to the observation that suggestions are negotiated differently, depending on the genre orientation of the participants.

The analysis of speech act episodes in the CANCODE corpus has shown that there are different ways to put forward a suggestion, such as 'respond to negative evaluation of other speaker', or 'provide information in support of one's own suggestion', as well as different ways of responding to and challenging suggestions. While such strategies have been described elsewhere (Brown & Levinson 1987; Banerjee & Carrell 1988), they have traditionally been described either at utterance level and/or by using some sort of elicitation method. Yet, Hinkel (1997) cautions that such methods may be unreliable and they may yield very different results to a corpus-based analysis. She argues that 'the ideal data for speech act analysis would consist of a large number of carefully recorded observations of particular speech acts' (1997:2). This chapter has illustrated how a corpus of spoken discourse might provide such data, and how it might be used to inform a corpus-based framework of individual speech act episodes.

CHAPTER 6

Pragmatic functions beyond the text

6.0 Introduction

The chapters in this book so far have focused on the analysis of transcribed conversations assembled in a corpus of spoken English. While the issues around the process of reducing what is essentially a multi-modal interaction to written mode are widely recognised, spoken corpus analysis to date has nevertheless relied heavily on transcribed data. In addition, spoken corpora are largely treated in the same way as their written counterparts when it comes to the analysis of lexical and grammatical patterns. The reason for this is mainly related to the additional cost and time involved in representing spoken interaction in any other form than a transcript. Yet, speech act expressions and corresponding speech act episodes rely as much on intonation and gesture in creating particular functions as they rely on the actual words and discourse structures that are being used. Since this book has been concerned with the development of a framework and a possible unit of meaning for studying speech acts in spoken corpora, this chapter highlights both the limitations of the descriptive apparatus discussed in previous chapters, and opportunities for extending the unit of analysis to include prosodic and gestural elements.

There are currently only few spoken corpus projects which embrace the painstaking annotation of spoken data with information on prosody and gesture, and which attempt to align audio and video streams with the transcript. The benefit of going through this process is substantial, not only in terms of discovering new patterns between the different modes, but also in terms of adding to the description and identification of patterns that have been derived on the basis of textual analysis of the transcripts.

Erman (2007), for example, studies pause frequency and pause duration in the London-Lund Corpus to ascertain whether these might be able to provide evidence for the size of linguistic units stored in the mental lexicon. She sees pauses as physical markers of how certain items are stored in the mental lexicon (see also Wood 2006). Similarly, Adolphs et al. (2006) analyse the placement of pauses in a corpus of learner English to test whether multi-word expressions that have been automatically extracted, are psycholinguistically valid. Both studies use audio data to complement and test textual analyses based on transcriptions of the same data.

In terms of the speech act expressions discussed in previous chapters, research on functional disambiguation in relation to intonation and pause patterns is pertinent. Van Lancker and Canter (1981) and Van Lancker, Canter and Terbeek (1981) study the effects of phonetic cues on the interpretation of ditropic sentences, i.e., sentences that can have either a literal or an idiomatic meaning (see also Ashby 2006). While the focus of these studies is mainly on conventional idioms, a prosodic analysis of speech act expressions in naturally occurring contexts would add an important dimension to their functional profiles. Differences in prosody in the expression *why don't you*, for example, will contribute to its reading as either a suggestion or a question. When it comes to spoken discourse, we tend to base our interpretation of utterance meaning at least partly on those elements which are not routinely captured in contemporary spoken corpora.

Apart from the use of the audio stream in spoken corpus analysis, access to video data of the recorded interactions is equally necessary for the description of patterns of meaning created in spoken discourse. This is because in spoken discourse, meaning is created through the interplay of different modalities (Kendon 1994; Kress & van Leeuwen 2001). And while current spoken corpora are some way off providing integrated interfaces that allow access to transcripts, sound and video, it is important to recognise that studies of pragmatic functions in spoken discourse require a multi-modal approach.

As outlined above, one of the problems with multi-modal corpus analysis is that the alignment and coding of naturally occurring interactions with different data-streams can be very time consuming. As a result, those corpora that include access to additional data-streams to the textual tend to be relatively small in size. It can therefore be difficult to derive enough instances of multi-modal patterns to make robust statements about their use. Rather than providing an extensive analysis of form/function composites in a multi-modal framework, this chapter will thus focus on the different issues involved in studying pragmatic functions in a multi-modal corpus, and discuss the implications for recording, representing and analysing multi-modal spoken corpora. In order to illustrate the relationship between the verbal and the visual, the pragmatic function of signalling active listenership is explored further. This function has been chosen because of the relatively explicit link between linguistic choices used as backchannels and their gestural counterparts, i.e. head-nods. While signals of active listenership have been studied extensively in terms of linguistic realisations and patterns, there is little empirical research on the interplay between the textual and the gestural components based on corpus data.

The discussion in this chapter thus focuses on illustrating the implications of multi-modal corpus development and analysis, and on the possible extensions and amendments that might have to be made to existing frameworks and analyses which are based solely on textual corpus evidence. In doing so, the chapter draws on research currently underway at the University of Nottingham which studies the representation and analysis of new forms of digital records, including multi-modal spoken corpora (see Adolphs & Carter 2007; Carter & Adolphs 2007; Adolphs et al. 2007). This research explores the role of new technologies and methodologies in the description and understanding of backchannels by addressing how participants in a converstaion utilise different modalities in order to position themselves towards the on-going subject matter.

6.1 Multi-modal communication

Early studies of communication where subjects were asked to participate in dyadic conversations while suppressing head, body and hand movements, showed that this task was next to impossible to achieve (Kendon 1980). The reason for this, as is now widely recognised, lies in the fact that naturally occurring communication relies on multiple modes of expression, on a combination of the verbal and the nonverbal, and on expressive signs, signals and cues or 'paralinguistic' features (Haiman 1998). In this respect, communication may be best described as operating within a complex network of direct and indirect 'semiotic channels' (Brown 1986) including, for example, patterns of *facial expression and gestures*, as well as intonation and vocabulary use.

Recent work in multi-modal communication has seen advances in both theory and practice. The theoretical starting point for much of the current work has been systemic-functional linguistics. *Systemic linguistics* is a theory that focuses on meaning, choice and probability in language, and on the significance of language as a social phenomenon, underlining how particular choices of word, grammar and structure encode different meanings in different contexts of language in use. Foundational work in multi-modal communication such as that advanced by Kress and van Leeuwen (1996), has illustrated how choices of image can align with verbal choices, and this work has been extended in recent years to embrace the multi-modal analyses of word, image and sound within different language varieties, including cartoons, comics, film, information leaflets, maps, advertisements (including TV advertisements), web pages and classroom textbooks (e.g. Baldry & Thibault 2004, 2006). The emphasis has been on how choices of one image or camera angle or colour tone can cumulatively encode particular meanings.

Work within a systemic-functional linguistic tradition does not always sit easily with corpus linguistic approaches. Often focused on single and mainly (but not exclusively) written texts, the former approach is concerned with establishing specific meanings in those texts, and with illustrating the integration of a theory of textual communication and qualitative methods of description, observation and insight. Corpus linguistic approaches seek more quantitative insights, are more concerned with regular, frequent and thus generalisable patterns of meaning and, while not atheoretical, embrace more empirical, practical methodologies for aligning word and meaning across a large number of texts.

, Work within Conversation Analysis (CA) has also explored descriptions of gestures and how these relate to the structure of talk. Schegloff (1984), for example, discusses hand gestures from a speaker and listener point of view, and lists various scenarios in which a non-speaker might use gestures in the negotiation for a turn. However, the focus of CA is firmly rooted in the analysis of transcripts rather than multi-modal records and as such the examples that are discussed are not normally supported by an analysis of patterns of gestures across large data samples stored in a corpus.

A particular challenge for current research is therefore to integrate the computer-enabled power of corpus linguistic methods with the theories and practices of multi-modal communication research, in other words, to provide computerised analyses of key patterns of meaning and to establish norms and regularities for these patterns. This would provide a basis for linking the verbal and the non-verbal in ways that allow new understandings of textuality to emerge.

6.1.1 Points of departure: From verbal to visual

Given the emphasis on verbal aspects of communication as captured in the form of transcripts in spoken corpora, it seems sensible to start with a feature that has already received some attention in terms of its distribution and realisation across different corpora. *Backchannels*, a term first coined by Yngve (1970), or signals of active listenership, lend themselves for further study in terms of the relationship between verbal and visual, as they can be studied in relation to a discrete set of gestural counterparts, i.e., head-nods. Head-nods, in turn, are recognised as one of the most salient gestures in communication. Head nods exist as part of a separate group of backchannels, consisting of non-vocalised, proxemic movement and kinesic signal. They are often viewed as one of the most highly conventionalised gestures of communication, and although not spoken, such gestures are integral in determining the meaning and function of talk as it unfolds. They provide means for hearers to register and to evaluate what is being said. Backchannels do not tend to feature in traditional accounts of speech acts which are more explicitly concerned with speaker turns than with listener turns. Yet, they carry an important pragmatic function and they are ubiquitous in spoken discourse. This means that an analysis of even a small corpus of spoken English should yield enough instances of backchannels for systematic analysis.

6.1.1.1 *Describing backchannels*

As identified by Sacks et al. (1974), turn-taking is a collaboratively organized achievement that exploits a complex 'social machinery' in its local accomplishment by speakers and hearers (Sacks 1992). In conversations listeners typically produce short utterances and non-verbal surrogates to indicate that they are following the speaker's turns. These 'accompaniment signals' are produced by the listener when the speaker is talking at length, and there is evidence that the speaker relies upon these for guidance as to how the message is being received (Kendon 1967). Observations of both verbal and non-verbal behaviour while listening (e.g. Goodwin 1981) tell us that listeners respond with precision at appropriate moments and in appropriate ways to incoming talk. Yngve (1970) introduced the term *backchannel* to refer to the 'short messages' that a speaker receives while holding the floor. He too points to the importance of these messages as markers of quality in ongoing communication. Yngve describes backchannels as a part of the process whereby a speaker who has the turn receives short messages, such as *yes* and *uh-huh*, from hearers without relinquishing the turn and as a means of signalling the hearer's active listenership (Yngve 1970; Roger & Nesshover 1987). Backchannels are not intended to take 'control of the floor', as a complete turn would, instead they invoke different communicative choices for the listener and are intended to offer 'relevant feedback' to the speaker (Mott & Petrie 1995).

There are a number of different forms that backchannels can take, including signalling acknowledgement and agreement as talk unfolds, marking 'newsworthy' items and declaring appreciation of a speaker's talk, clarifying the sense and meaning of an utterance (in this respect, something like *uh?* may prompt further talk on the speaker's part to make his or her meaning clear). Backchannels may also include laughter, sighs and other sympathetic messages that signal the hearer's active listenership (Maynard 1989, 1990, 1997; Schegloff 1982; Gardner 1997, 1998, 2002).

Although, on a basic level, head-nods adopt the same highly conventionalised, and to some extent, easily definable 'form', namely that of up and down motion of the head, their given meaning in discourse is not straightforward. Just like their verbal counterparts, they do not have just one specific *function*. In the same way as the meaning of vocalisations (*eh, hmm, uh-huh*, etc.) depends on the situation, so too does the meaning of head-nods and other bodily gestures. The use of head-nods in conversation extends beyond the most common connotations of affirmation and negation (McClave 2000), and includes deictic forms that are 'directly related to the discourse structure of an utterance' (Kendon 1972). Head nods are, in other words, vital ingredients in conversational production, maintenance and management. In the terms of systemic-functional linguistics and studies within a multi-modal tradition, they invoke different communicative choices and vary according to different social environments and different social relations of the speakers.

A wide range of terms and definitions are available to describe the functions of backchannels, and there is a growing body of research which shows that backchannels have more than one macro function (e.g., Schegloff 1982; Maynard 1989). Research findings have shown that gestures such as head-nods can act as a substitute for speech (Goldin-Meadow 1999). However, misunderstandings occur as a result of a variety of factors, including a lack of substantive information held by the recipient of the message, which is particularly common where cultural differences occur, and intentional or unintentional mismatches between gestures and the spoken word. Furthermore, while verbal and non-verbal backchannels complement and regulate each other (Brown 1986), they do not necessarily do so in a consistent way throughout the conversation, even with the same participants. For example, at any given point, a head-nod may be used in conjunction with *yeah* to mark agreement or convergence, but elsewhere the head-nod alone may mark the convergence, without an accompanying vocalisation. Conversely, a different gesture used in conjunction with the same utterance does not always generate a different meaning within a specific conversation.

The conditional relevance of backchannels is also specific to the subjects involved and the topics of conversation. This does not mean, however, that gestural backchannels are idiosyncratic. Rather, they display standardized (Kendon 1996) and 'emblematic' qualities (McClave 2000), which are specific to a channel, use and function at a specific time and place. In short, while subject to exigencies of the situation, gestural backchannels (like verbal backchannels) are part and parcel of our equipment for organizing and accomplishing talk (Sacks et al. 1974). The situated character of backchannels – their manifestation in the 'here and now', in just this place, at just this time, with just these people – can make the detection, exploration and analysis of stable patterns difficult. However, it is important to develop our abilities to 'read' them in terms of their situated functions, when and where they occur in context and co-text, to provide the foundations of a more complete understanding of the real time character of discourse (Goldin-Meadow 1999).

To explore head-nods in conversation thus requires the ability to monitor the function, timing, significance and response (if any) of parties to a conversation. The research reported here explores the development of a tool which aims to enable the development of multi-modal corpora, and support the exploration of verbal *and* visual data within the same frame of reference. The tool offers the potential to open up the complexities of multi-modal communication, and to develop a foundation for unpacking active listenership, backchannel construction, and comprehension. Through an initial explication of head-nods, the aim is to provide the basis for a broader methodological approach for detecting, exploring, annotating and analysing the interplay between talk and gestures through the aligned representation of video and verbal data from conversational exchanges.

6.1.1.2 *Corpus-based analyses of backchannels*

Previous research on backchannels in corpora has looked at the distribution of both forms and functions of individual backchannels across different contexts and different varieties of English (see for example O'Keeffe & Adolphs forthcoming; McCarthy 2003). In their analysis O'Keeffe and Adolphs find, for example, that there are inter-varietal differences between the two corpora they study in that there are distributional inconsistencies, both in terms of forms and functions of backchannels in the Irish and British English corpus.

Table 6.1 O'Keeffe and Adolphs' (forthcoming) framework for classification and functions of backchannels

Type of token	Function	Typical examples
Continuer tokens	Maintain the flow of the discourse.	Minimal forms such as *Yeah, mm.*
Convergence tokens	Markers of agreement/convergence. They are linked to points in the discourse: 1) where there is a topic boundary or closure 2) where there is a need to converge on an understanding of what is *common ground* or shared knowledge between participants.	Many forms can perform this function such as: – single word items *yeah* – follow-up questions such as *did you?is she?* – short statements, e.g. agreeing statements *yeah it's pretty sad.*
Engagement tokens	Markers of high engagement where addressee(s) respond on an affective level to the content of the message. These backchannels express genuine emotional responses such as surprise, shock, horror, sympathy, empathy and so on.	They manifest in many forms for example: – single-word forms such as *excellent, absolutely* – short statements and repetitions *that's nice, oh wow, oh really* – follow-up questions *did you?*
Information receipt tokens	Markers of points in the discourse where adequate information has been received. These responses can impose a boundary in the discourse and can signal a point of topic transition or closure, and they can be indicative of asymmetrical discourse.	*Right* and *okay*

A wealth of research exists that is concerned with the different functions of backchannels in discourse, and a number of corpus-based studies have used existing classifications (such as Schegloff 1982; McCarthy 2002; Maynard 1989) as the basis for the development of frameworks that could be applied to corpus data.

The different functions in Table 6.1 mirror different levels of engagements of the hearer in the on-going conversation. The following extracts taken from Adolphs (2006) illustrates some of the core functions outlined in Table 6.1. In the first extract three cleaners in a university hall of residence discuss the cleaning of student bedrooms. Speakers 2 and 1 signal that they are listening to speaker 3 through the use of a range of different backchannel vocalisations which indicate varying degrees of involvement.

<S03> Well the fridge probably was+
<S02> <unintelligible>
<S03> +cos I mean I I didn't clean the fridge.
<S02> Yeah. But it can be bad an hour after.
<S03> But I er I cleaned <S0=> all the <\S0=> all the thing and mopped all
    the floors+
<S02> **Mm.**
<S03> +in the morning. I mean what annoys me it puts you off doing any-
    thing.
<S01> **Mhm.**
<S03> What annoys me is that if a student comes up to me and says Can
    you clean tomorrow or Can you clean an <S0=> hour <\S0=> half an
    hour later. And you turn round and you say Yes.
<S01> **Mhm.**
<S03> And then the problem with it is you're willing to do something for
    them.
<S01> **Yeah.**
<S02> And then what do they do for you?
<S01> Nothing.
<S03> **No.**

In this extract there are instances of simple continuers (*Mhm*, *Mm*) and convergence tokens (*Yeah*, *No*). Examples of more engaged response tokens can be found in the next extract from Adolphs (2006) in which two female teachers discuss the way in which one of their fellow teacher deals with a difficult class of pupils:

<S02> There's one or two as I say nasty elements you know in there. <S0=> And they seem and </S0=> But Seven E H I know Annie teaches them and er cos she had them in a while for P S E. And sh= you know she was tearing her hair out with them.

<S01> **Really.**

<S02> Mm. I mean she's an ex deputy head yet she'd had+

<S01> <S0=> Erm I think </S0=>

<S02> +enough as well by the end of term. <S0E> laughs </S0E> <S0=> And I thought God if </S0=>

<S01> I think that gets Maggie down as well cos she <unintelligible>.

<S0E> laughs </S0E>

<S02> **That's right.**

<S01> She's very keen.

<S02> **Absolutely.**

<S01> And she gets fed up when they're being+

<S02> **I would.**

<S01> +told off all day.

<S02> **I would.** After this term with sort of total mixed ability for French I would just have a sink class quite honestly. And apparently this Mrs Thompson who's coming she she wants to stream for French or set them for French.

In this extract the response tokens such as *really* and *absolutely*, as well as multi-word sequences such as *that's right* mark a more engaged style of listenership and would thus fall under the category of *engagement tokens* in Table 6.1.

While this basic categorisation scheme can be a useful starting point for analysing verbal realisations of backchannels, the question of how verbal and visual realisations interact within and across such categories has remained largely under-explored. Verbal and non-verbal backchannels may vary according to their placement (i.e. the specific point(s) in discourse in which they occur), intensity and duration, and we therefore need to identify 'shared' groupings or categories which take into account these multi-modal characteristics. In order to develop an understanding of the nature of such shared groupings, we need to explore different techniques for detecting, coding and replaying visual and verbal elements of backchannels in a multi-modal corpus.

6.1.1.3 *Merging verbal and visual*

The main challenge for developing support for the analysis of multi-modal corpora is the need for an *integrated* approach to the representation of data. There is a basic requirement to create tools that support the 'marking up' or identification of multi-modal patterns and the subsequent codification of recognizable patterns. A number of coding schemes exist for marking up verbal aspects of talk including the one outlined above in relation to backchannels. Coding schemes for mark-ing up non-verbal elements, on the other hand, are not as widely used within the applied linguistic community and, as a result, the specific requirements of such schemes that allow the encoding of gestures, facial expressions, gaze, head and body movement, posture etc. for the purpose of linguistic analysis still need to be articulated.

One common coding strategy used in systems of facial gesture and movement recognition is the Facial Animation Coding System (*FACS*). This system was de-veloped by Ekman and Friesen (1975) to create an easy to use reference system that could be used to code and classify facial expressions. *FACS* is an automated tracking system which defines specific head and facial expression movements in accordance with sequences of motion of 46 different action units (AUs) for facial expression, and 12 separate ones for head orientation and gaze. Once the AUs are defined, they are used as input into a Hidden Markov Model which classifies gen-erative movements statistically. However, *FACS* is unable to encode verbal data, being designed to deal with visual data only. There is a need, then, to develop integrated coding schemes for verbal and visual data.

In order to be able to use corpus linguistic techniques to analyse patterns in language, it becomes even more important that codes are consistently applied across the whole corpus. This is because automated extraction of patterns relies on consistent representation of verbal and visual phenomena. The usability of multi-modal coding schemes is a key issue to consider at this early stage of de-velopment. Coding schemes need to be developed in such a way that they can be shared across different communities of practice which are likely to have different representational and analytical needs.

In order to apply codes to data, new tools have to be developed that allow cod-ing of verbal and non-verbal elements of naturally occurring interaction, and that provide mechanisms for the extraction of patterns and alignment of data-streams. One such interface is DRS (Digital Replay System) which is currently being de-veloped at the University of Nottingham (see Greenhalgh et al. 2007) and builds on the earlier ReplayTool software (see French et al. 2006). DRS is being devel-oped to assist in the exploration of digital records including for the purpose of ethnographic enquiry (Crabtree et al. 2005) and linguistic description (Adolphs & Carter 2007).

The Digital Replay System allows video data to be imported and aligned. The transcript can be annotated and be played alongside the video and audio stream. Further analytical annotations can be added such as those that encode a partic-ular gesture. The annotation mechanism provides an initial means for marking up multi-modal data and for maintaining the coherence between spoken lan-guage and accompanying gestural elements or 'phrases' (Kendon 1996; Kirk et al. 2005). DRS also includes a concordance viewer as illustrated in Figure 6.1 and

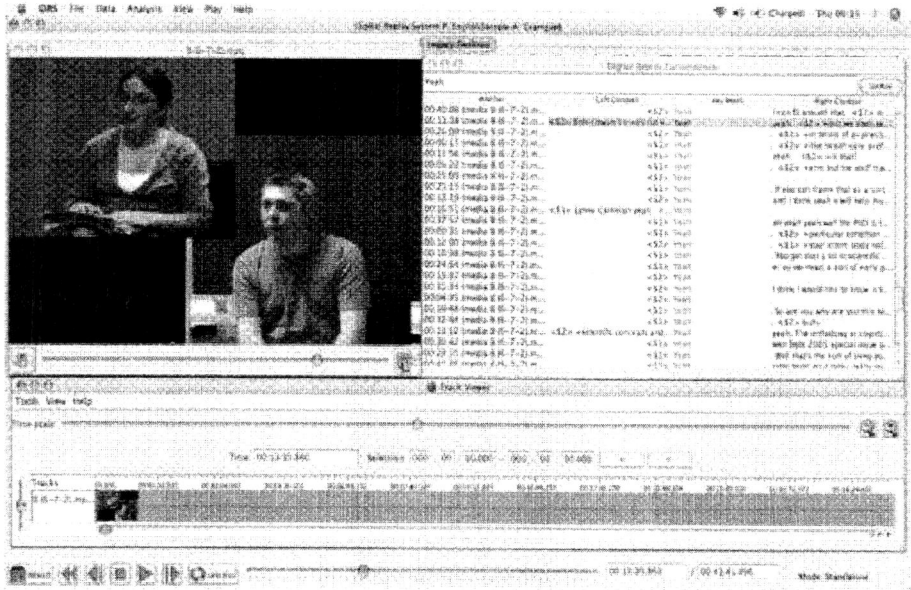

Figure 6.1 Screenshot of Digital Replay System

provides the analyst with different points of entry into the data. An initial search of particular *backchannel* items, such as *yeah*, generates all of the instances of this *backchannel* in the corpus. Individual concordance lines give further access to the position in the transcript where the item occurs and the corresponding place in the video. A study of corresponding patterns between verbal and visual thus becomes possible.

6.2 Head-nods and backchannels: An integrated approach

While there is a level of interpretation when it comes to transcribing spoken discourse, the textual element of the listenership episode is relatively easy to establish and patterns of common backchannels can be extracted from existing multi-million word corpora. These types of patterns have been linked to particular functions in the area of corpus linguistics as outlined above. Yet, the accompanying head movement, as well as the intonation pattern, can change the function of the backchannel realisation, which in turn affects the surrounding discourse. It is therefore important to be able to establish some way of recognising the visual elements in a *principled way* so that these can be studied in relation to the verbal elements without adding a burdensome layer of interpretative intervention to the initial representation of the data. There is, then, a need to develop techniques for recognising gestures automatically and that work *across utterances* to reduce the overall interpretative element in the extraction of verbal-visual patterns from the corpus.

Carter and Adolphs (2007) illustrate a possible multi-modal approach to analysing active listenership in an academic supervision session. Their analysis of head-nods is based on classifications established with the use of computer-vision techniques. They identify five broad types of head-nods:

Type A: small (low amplitude) nods with short duration
Type B: small (low amplitude), multiple nods with a longer duration than type A
Type C: intense (high amplitude) nods with a short duration
Type D: intense and multiple nods with a longer duration than type C
Type E: multiple nods, comprising of a combination of types A and C, with a longer duration than types A and C.

Using the functional categories in the O'Keeffe and Adolphs (forthcoming) framework outlined above in conjunction with the different head-nod types, Carter and Adolphs (2007) carry out a preliminary analysis of a 10 minute stretch of video extracted from an MA supervision session. This session is pictured in the DRS screenshot in Figure 6.2. They analyse the backchannels used by the supervisor who uses 40 verbal backchannels in total, of which 18 are accompanied by a nod and 22 are purely verbal. In addition, the supervisor uses 24 nods which are not accompanied by a verbal signal.

Focusing initially on the verbal backchannels, they find that the supervisor uses 11 continuers, 9 convergence tokens, 14 information receipt tokens, and 6 engaged response tokens. In terms of the types of head-nods used by the supervisor, the data breaks down as follows: Type A (13), Type B (13), Type C (12), Type D (2), Type E (2). In a final step those instances where a verbal backchannel is accompanied by a head-nod are examined. This analysis shows that half of the small nods of short duration (type A) co-occurred with the information receipt function, while half of the small nods of longer duration (type B) co-occurred with the function of a convergence token. All of the type C nods (i.e. short and intense nods) used by the supervisor are accompanied by a verbal signal which has been classified as carrying either the 'continuer' or 'convergence' function.

As with the speech act episodes discussed in the previous chapter, it is important to take a discourse level perspective when analysing active listenership. Head-nods, as well as the verbal backchannels, occur in a particular place in relation to the main speaker's utterance and their function is likely to be related to the place in which they occur. More data is needed to establish the nature of the relationship between head-nods and verbal backchannels. For now, it is important to note that gestures form a key part of the speech act episode and need to be included in any comprehensive analysis of human communication in use.

One of the main issues in multi-modal corpus analysis and representation is that corpus linguistics has traditionally focused on discrete items, such as individual words or grammatical categories. The complexities of gesture and movement, on the other hand, mean that such units do not lend themselves to be studied alongside traditional units of analysis. Baldry and Thibault (2006: 181p) point out that it is 'critically important [...] that corpus-based approaches to text engage with the level of discourse analysis and discourse-level meaning relations on various scalar levels of textual organisation'. While the integration of scalar levels and discrete categories is likely to cause problems in the development of an integrated framework, it also promises a much richer description of patterns in social interactions.

6.3 Summary

The research presented in this chapter has shown how the analysis of pragmatic functions in naturally occurring spoken discourse might be supported by the use of a multi-modal corpus resource. The analysis of backchannels in relation to head-nods illustrates that a purely textual type of analysis can only ever lead to an incomplete description of how meaning is negotiated. It has further shown that any categorisation scheme of pragmatic functions that is based on transcripts alone, might have to be reconsidered in the light of the kind of evidence we can draw from the visual elements of collaborative interaction.

The development of multi-modal corpora is in its early stages and further developments with regard to recording, representing and coding naturally occurring data are required if spoken corpus analysis is to benefit from a multi-modal approach. As outlined above, a particular challenge in this context will be the integration of verbal and visual categories. While corpus linguistics to date works with relatively discrete categories, gestures cannot be described and categorised in the same way. They are dynamic in nature and whether a head-nod, for example, is judged to be of high or low intensity, is currently very much the judgement call of the analyst who decides on the parameters for such categories. So while this kind of research allows us to extend our descriptions of discourse and to evaluate some of the categories we have developed for individual pragmatic functions based on textual data, it also requires careful consideration of whether full analytical integration of two systems which are vastly different in nature is possible.

The technology has advanced to a point where the alignment of multi-modal data streams has become possible, and fully searchable multi-modal spoken corpora are now becoming available. The applications of such a database are many and varied, and the study of natural language is a focus in a diverse range of disciplines. However, the challenges of conceptualising and theorising the search for patterns that bridge the verbal and the visual in a multi-modal spoken corpus are still to be addressed in a systematic way.

CHAPTER 7

Concluding remarks

7.0 Opportunities and limitations of spoken corpus analysis

The research reported in this book has been concerned with outlining the scope of using spoken corpora as the basis for studying pragmatic functions. Using as an example the speech act *suggestion* it was illustrated how a corpus might be used to provide evidence for the description of functions in use. A shift in focus from literal versus non-literal interpretations of speech act expressions to the development of functional profiles based on corpus evidence was proposed in Chapters 3 and 4. The research reported here is broadly in line with other corpus studies which have developed new frameworks for analysing meaning based on actual language in use. Recurring patterns are used as evidence for the relationship between form and meaning, and a description of functional profiles of the speech act expressions discussed in this volume ultimately rests on this relationship.

A corpus-based description allows us to distinguish between speech act expressions which appear to be functionally synonymous, such as *why don't you* and *why not* for example, in terms of their contextual distribution, their collocations, and the place where they occur in the on-going discourse. It further allows us to test existing theories and claims about such expressions made on an intuitive basis with very little data or data that is not naturally occurring. For example, in a discussion of gambits Keller (1979) argues that '[s]everal gambits are marked for use with a single listener; for example a suggestion offered to an audience of one could take the form "If I were you", while with a larger audience, the unmarked form *Why not...* might be used' (1979: 230). Access to a spoken corpus which includes comprehensive contextual information affords an empirical evaluation of such claims. A spoken corpus can thus provide evidence not only for more robust descriptions of pragmatic functions in use, but also for testing and evaluating existing theories and claims made about the way in which they are used.

In addition, access to the discourse environment in which individual functions are used further allows for the description of discourse structural patterns in relation to individual speech act expressions. And further developments of spoken corpora which include audio and video data aligned with transcripts, offer a new perspective on the interactions between different modalities when it comes to performing and describing particular pragmatic functions.

There are a number of issues to bear in mind when it comes to the analysis of pragmatic functions in spoken corpora, and to the evaluation of the outcomes of such research. As outlined in Chapter 2, a corpus-based approach limits the point of entry into the data to a particular form and, as a result, the extraction of comprehensive lists of individual functions is not easily achieved with such an approach. In addition, pragmatic functions are highly context dependent and while we can attempt to categorise and analyse different contexts and text-types, the more delicate variations in context are impossible to capture systematically. It is further unlikely that speakers and listeners are predictable in the way in which they choose to negotiate pragmatic functions in on-going discourse to the extent that all of the possible variations and patterns could be fully described. This applies in particular to un-scripted discourse such as in the extracts of casual conversation discussed in this book.

As already outlined in previous chapters, spoken corpora are distinctly different to written corpora, yet they are often analysed in the same way. This is a problem because of the implicit assumption that the two are comparable types of assembled records which can be analysed with the same methods and frameworks. Spoken corpora have been rendered into written form and are therefore already analysed to a certain extent. This analysis is mainly related to the kinds of decisions taken during the transcription process and the degree of delicacy applied to the way in which certain aspects of the talk are represented, such as speaker changes, overlaps, pauses, etc. The fact that naturally occurring conversation happens along a time line during which several things might co-occur makes it difficult to represent such interactions in the form of a transcript which is essentially linear in format. This in turn may impact on the results of our analyses.

The issue of how best to represent spoken discourse, and the fact that detailed transcriptions are very time consuming, leads to another important difference between spoken and written corpora: their size. In order to collect enough evidence for robust descriptions of individual lexico-grammatical constructions, it is necessary to have a large corpus. The analyses in this book are based on relatively small data samples and the main aim has been to outline possible ways of using spoken corpora to study pragmatic functions. Larger spoken corpora, carefully annotated in terms of contextual information and transcribed to a high degree of delicacy, are required to test the approach and hypotheses outlined in this volume.

There is a distinct tension then between the need to create accurate records of spoken interactions and the need to build spoken corpora that are large enough to support the kinds of questions one might want to ask about the use of pragmatic functions.

The fact that spoken interaction is multi-modal in nature, as discussed in the last chapter, and that meaning in interaction is created through the interplay of verbal language and body language, complicates matters further. In using frameworks designed for the analysis of written corpora to describe pragmatic functions in spoken corpora, we ignore aspects of intonation and gesture. There are, of course, certain areas of investigation which are less likely to depend on the interaction between different modalities, such as the study of grammatical patterns or frequency distributions of individual words and phrases, for example. And it could be argued that gesture is merely supportive of talk, and that we should be able to arrive at a comprehensive description of spoken discourse by referring to transcribed records alone. However, it will ultimately be difficult to sustain a mode of analysis that disregards at least two of the key components in meaning creation.

7.1 Possible areas of application

Drawing on a corpus of spoken discourse for the analysis of pragmatic functions has relevance for language description, as well as for a wide range of applied contexts, notably English language teaching and learning, and translation studies.

Schmidt and Richards (1980) point out that the effective performance of speech acts forms part of the 'communicative competence' (Hymes 1972, 1973; Munby 1978) of a speaker. They argue:

> 'While the concept of communicative competence is not new, much remains to be done to substantiate the concept empirically, and the study of the role of speech acts in second language learning could make a useful contribution to our knowledge of how second and foreign languages are acquired' (1980: 141).

In a similar vein McCarthy (1998) highlights that the communicative approach to language teaching has led to 'an overly simplistic tendency to equate speech-acts with particular linguistic formulae, a sort of "phrasicon" of speech acts, or "functions", as they were often popularly called, and there was a tendency simply to invent such formulae rather than examine real data' (1998: 19). A shift in focus towards a communicative approach in ELT has thus created a particular need for context-sensitive descriptions of pragmatic functions, and a corpus-based analysis of such functions might provide useful evidence in this context.

In terms of translation studies, the speech act expressions described in this book have long been a key site of analysis. Platinga (1987: 37), quoted in Thibault and van Leeuwen (1996), argues that:

> Out of the scrap heap of sentences rejected by a literal interpreter, we now need ways to process non-literal but still meaningful sentences. In addition to figurative language, non-literal language includes speech acts, both direct and indirect. The canonical example of a speech act is: 'Can you pass the salt?' The appropriate response to this utterance is neither [sic] the act of passing the salt nor an expla-

nation of why this task cannot be completed. An inappropriate response would be yes or no.

Corpus analysis has already established itself as a useful tool for establishing translation equivalence (see for example Tognini-Bonelli & Manca 2004), and the description of functional profiles of individual speech act expressions could be used as a possible framework to further support such work.

7.2 The role of context

The earlier chapters in this book have dealt with the categorisation of context in relation to speech act expressions. Access to spoken corpora which have been categorised in terms of contextual parameters, however these are identified, offer a unique opportunity to study contextual distributions of linguistic choices. This, it was argued, affords better descriptions of pragmatic functions as the contextual configurations in interactions are recognised to be of key importance in determining the level of directness applied to individual speech acts. Yet, the research in this book has shown that wider contextual categories are not sufficient to determine levels of directness, but that these have to be linked with descriptions of the immediate discourse environment of a particular speech act expression. A possible framework for analysing speech act episodes based on corpus examples was introduced in Chapter 5.

One of the main issues with the description of context, both in terms of the wider context of the situation and in terms of the immediate discourse context, is that in naturally occurring discourse, context is highly dynamic and affected by ever changing goals of the participants. While corpus data can provide evidence for possible patterns of the relationship between goal-types, discourse structure and speech act expression, this kind of pattern cannot be extracted in an automated fashion. It relies on the development and application of complex frameworks which have to be tested with every new interaction that is being studied.

The boundaries between corpus analysis, which is traditionally associated with at least some form of automated process of extracting instances of a specified form and discourse analysis, become blurred in this process. This is not a problem as such and there is now a body of research which illustrates how the two disciplines might benefit from one another (see, for example, Baker 2006 and McCarthy 1998). However, the effects on the status of the research results when automated procedures are combined with frameworks and categories, which have emerged through prior analysis and are based on preconceived ideas about context, need to be further explored. It is therefore important to be as explicit as possible about the rationale for defining discoursal and contextual categories for spoken corpus design and analysis.

7.3 Future challenges

The discussion in this volume has started with a description of one of the key issues in speech act theory: the interpretation of utterance meaning in relation to the lexico-grammatical strings used by the speaker. With a growing body of research in corpus linguistics and increasing interest in corpus-based pragmatics, one of the main challenges in this area is to define a unit of analysis for pragmatic functions. Studies of corpora consisting of hundreds of millions of words have started to show that the word as the unit of meaning has to be re-evaluated, and Sinclair (1996) illustrates how other patterns including collocation and grammatical integration of a word form part of its unit of meaning. At the same time, corpus-based work on multi-word expressions highlights their ubiquity in language use (e.g. Schmitt 2004) which further supports the necessity of a re-evaluation of traditional models of lexis and grammar. As far as speech act theory is concerned, the analysis of speech act expressions in a corpus appears to be a good starting point to study the interface between semantics and pragmatics, especially in relation to the notion of literal versus non-literal meaning. This has been illustrated in Chapters 2 and 3. However, as far as spoken corpora are concerned, there is still a need to find a suitable unit of analysis, and it is unlikely that a concordance output will suffice in the description of pragmatic functions. Instead, a corpus that tries to capture the collaborative and dynamic nature of naturally occurring discourse is required for an exploration of a more stable unit that includes descriptions at the level of the utterance, discourse, and context. Some possible ways in which such a framework might be developed have been discussed in this book but there is a need for further research on the interaction between spoken corpus design, analytical frameworks used and the status of emerging results of any analysis.

Another major challenge lies in the development of spoken corpora that are large enough to support the description of pragmatic functions. As outlined above, a sensible way of balancing detailed transcription with developing large data-sets has to be established. With advances in voice recognition software and automated transcription this task might become easier in future. However, it is important to resist the temptation of altering the settings and contexts in order to make such technology usable. The question of what is 'naturally occurring' for the purpose of assembling spoken corpora is a key issue, and the way in which we record such interactions and the sites at which we record them have a direct impact on the discourse itself.

Finally, there are substantial challenges in recording, representing and replaying multi-modal spoken data as discussed in Chapter 6. These are related both to the development of theories that help account for multi-modal interaction in terms of recurring patterns that we can derive from a corpus, and to the technical issues of making video recordings in natural contexts and aligning the resulting records in a way that allows the text, audio and video to be analysed in a systematic way. These issues are likely to become more complex as the use of mobile technology blurs the boundaries between speech and writing, and some of the most interesting challenges for the analysis of pragmatic functions might lie in the development of frameworks that account for the kind of fragmented discourses that emerge from the interface of human and computer interaction in real contexts. Building corpora that provide evidence to support the analysis of new situated forms of interaction will remain a challenge and is likely to require substantial interdisciplinary collaboration to be successful.

Transcription conventions for the CANCODE data used in this book

Transcription conventions of spoken interactions vary depending on the research purpose of the respective project for which they are used. For a corpus of spoken discourse to be re-usable by other researchers, the transcription has to be as extensive as possible. Yet, even when great care is taken to achieve an accurate representation of the recorded interaction, textual renderings of spoken interaction can never provide a completely accurate picture of the event. This is due to a number of reasons, some of which relate to the multi-modal nature of spoken discourse which is not easily represented in existing spoken corpora. Other reasons relate to the fact that there is always a level of interpretation involved in any type of transcription.

The table below serves as a guide to the transcription conventions and codes used for the CANCODE corpus. The transcriptions of the CANCODE corpus do not include prosodic information. Some parts of the corpus have been coded for overlapping speech while others have not. For the purpose of this book the original transcription conventions have been kept for some of the extracts and concordance lines, while in other extracts some of the codes have been deleted to aid ease of reading.

Transcription convention	Symbol	Explanation
Speaker codes	<S01>, <S02>, <S0F>, <S0M>	Each speaker is numbered with separate codes. Where it has been impossible to identify a particular speaker, which is sometimes the case in conversations with many different speakers, the transcriber has indicated whether the speaker was male <S0M> or female <S0F>.
Extralinguistic information	<$E>...</$E>	This includes laughter, coughs and transcribers' comments about speech on the tape, including notes on anonymised elements, e.g. <$E> company name </$E>

Transcription convention	Symbol	Explanation
Unintelligible speech	<G?>, <G1>	Unintelligible speech is marked with these brackets. Where the number of unintelligible syllables can be determined, this is indicated within the tag, e.g. <G1>, <G2>, etc. Where this number cannot be determined the transcriber has used the symbol <G?>
Guess	<$H>...</$H>	Where the accuracy of the transcription is uncertain, the sequence of words in question is placed between these two angle brackets.
Interrupted sentence	+	When an utterance is interrupted by another speaker this is indicated by using a + sign at the end of the interrupted utterance and at the point where the speaker resumes his or her utterance: <S 01> You could + <S 02> Yeah <S 01> + come round tonight
Overlap	<$O1>...</$O1>	Some parts of the corpus have been coded for overlapping speech. For this purpose the overlap is indicated by numbered angle brackets: <$O1>...</$O1>, <$O2>...</$O2> <S02> Oh. So I'll have to re-calibrate those <$O1> then <\$O1>? <S01> <$O1> Yes. <\$O1> I'm afraid <$O2> so. You will have <\$O2> <S02> <$O2> Oh. Will it <\$O2> not take the previous calibration?
Unfinished sentence, repeat, or false start	<$=>...</$>	Unfinished sentences of any type are placed between these angle brackets. This type of coding aids subsequent parsing procedures performed on the data, as well as analyses of patterns of spoken grammar in the corpus.
Punctuation	. ?	A full stop or question mark is used to mark the end of a sentence (depending on intonation). 'Sentences' are anything that is felt to be a complete utterance, such as: <S02> Erm is MX there? <S01> He's got somebody with him at the moment MX. <S02> Right. 'Right' is considered as a sentence here. Unfinished sentences are not followed by a full stop.

References

Adolphs, S. 2001. Linking Lexico-grammar and Speech Acts: A Corpus-based Approach. PhD dissertation, The University of Nottingham.

Adolphs, S. 2006. *Introducing Electronic Text Analysis: A Practical Guide for Language and Literary Studies.* Abingdon: Routledge.

Adolphs, S., Brown, B., Carter, R., Crawford, P. & Sahota, O. 2004. Applying corpus linguistics in a health care context. *Journal of Applied Linguistics 1: 9–28.*

Adolphs, S., Dahlmann, I. & Rodden, T. 2006. Investigating the use of pauses as an indicator of holistic storage of multi-word units (MWUs) in spoken learner language. Paper presented at the 39th annual meeting of the British Association of Applied Linguistics, 7–9 September 2006, University College, Cork, Ireland.

Adolphs, S., Bertenthal, B., Boker, S., Carter, R., Greenhalgh, C., Herald, M., Kenny, S, Levow, G., Papke, M. & Pridmore, T. 2007. *Integrating cyberinfrastructure into existing e-social science research*, Online Proceedings of the 3rd International Conference on e-Social Science, October 7–9, Ann Arbor, MI: ESRC/NSF. http://ess.si.umich.edu

Adolphs, S. & Carter, R. 2007. Beyond the word: New challenges in analysing corpora of spoken English. *European Journal of English Studies* 11(2): 114–128.

Aijmer, K. 1984. Sort of and kind of in English conversation. *Studia Linguistica* 38: 118–128.

Aijmer, K. 1986. Discourse variation and hedging. In *Corpus Linguistics* II: *New Studies in the Analysis and Exploitation of Computer Corpora*, J. Aarts & W. Meijs (eds), 1–18. Amsterdam: Rodopi.

Aijmer, K. 1996. *Conversational Routines in English.* London: Longman.

Aijmer, K. 2002. *English Discourse Particles: Evidence from a Corpus.* Amsterdam: John Benjamins.

Alexander, R. J. 1984. Fixed expressions in English: Reference books and the teacher. *English Language Teaching Journal* 38: 127–134.

Ashby, M. 2006. Prosody and idioms in English. *Journal of Pragmatics* 38: 1580–1597.

Askehave, I. & Swales, J. M. 2001. Genre, identification and communicative purpose: A problem and a possible solution. *Applied Linguistics* 22: 195–212.

Aston, G. & Burnard, L. 1998. *The BNC Handbook: Exploring the British National Corpus with SARA.* Edinburgh: EUP.

Austin, J. L. 1962. *How to Do Things with Words.* Oxford: Clarendon Press.

Bach, K. & Harnish, R. M. 1979. *Linguistic Communication and Speech Acts.* Cambridge MA: The MIT Press.

Baker, P. 2006. *Using Corpora in Discourse Analysis.* London: Continuum.

Bakhtin, M. M. 1986. The problem of speech in genres. In *Speech Genres and Other Late Essays*, C. Emersen & M. Holquist (eds), 60–102. Austin TX: University of Texas Press.

Baldry, A. & Thibault, P. J. 2004. *Multimodal Transcription and Text Analysis.* London: Equinox.

Baldry, A. & Thibault, P. J. 2006. Multimodal corpus linguistics. In *System and Corpus: Exploring Connections*, G. Thompson & S. Hunston (eds), 164–183. London: Equinox.

Banerjee, J. & Carrell, P. L. 1988. Tuck in your shirt, you squid: Suggestions in ESL. *Language Learning* 38: 313–364.

Bardovi-Harlig, K. & Hartford, B. S. 1990. Congruence in native and nonnative conversations: Status balance in the academic advising session. *Language Learning* 40: 467–501.

Barron, A. 2003. *Acquisition in Interlanguage Pragmatics*. Amsterdam: John Benjamins.

Bhatia, V. K. 1993. *Analysing Genre: Language Use in Professional Settings*. London: Longman.

Biber, D. 1988. *Variation across Speech and Writing*. Cambridge: CUP.

Biber, D. 1989. A typology of English texts. *Linguistics* 27(3): 3–43.

Biber, D. & Finegan, E. 1986. An initial typology of English text types. In *Corpus Linguistics* II: *New Studies in the Analysis and Exploitation of Computer Corpora*, J. Aarts & W. Meijs (eds), 19–46. Amsterdam: Rodopi.

Biber, D. & Finegan, E. 1989. Styles of stance in English: Lexical and grammatical marking of evidentiality and affect. *Text* 9(1): 93–124.

Biber, D., Conrad, S. & Reppen, R. 1998. *Corpus Linguistics: Investigating Language Structure and Use*. Cambridge: CUP.

Biber, D., Johansson, S., Leech, G., Conrad, S. & Finegan, E. 1999. *Longman Grammar of Spoken and Written English*. London: Pearson.

Blum-Kulka, S. 1982. Learning to say what you mean in a second language: A study of speech act performance of learners of Hebrew as a second language. *Applied Linguistics* 3: 29–59.

Blum-Kulka, S. 1987. Indirectness and politeness in requests: Same or different? *Journal of Pragmatics* 11: 131–146.

Blum-Kulka, S. 1989. Playing it safe: The role of conventionality and indirectness. In *Cross-cultural Pragmatics: Requests and Apologies*, S. Blum-Kulka, J. House & G. Kasper (eds), 37–70. Norwood NJ: Ablex.

Blum-Kulka, S., House, J. & Kasper, G. 1989. Investigating cross-cultural pragmatics: An introductory overview. In *Cross-cultural Pragmatics: Requests and Apologies*, S. Blum-Kulka, J. House & G. Kasper (eds), 1–34. Norwood NJ: Ablex.

Bolton, K., Nelson, G. & Hung, J. (2003). A corpus-based study of connectors in student writing: Research from the International Corpus of English in Hong Kong (ICE-HK). *International Journal of Corpus Linguistics 7(2): 165–182*.

Brown, G. & Yule, G. 1983. *Discourse Analysis*. Cambridge: CUP.

Brown, P. & Levinson, S. C. 1987. *Politeness: Some Universals in Language Usage*. Cambridge: CUP.

Brown, P. & Levinson, S. 1987. *Politeness: Some Universals in Language Usage*. Cambridge: CUP.

Brown, R. 1986. *Social Psychology*, 2nd edn. New York NY: Free Press.

Bühler, K. 1934/1990. *Sprachtheorie. Die Darstellungsfunktion der Sprache. /Theory of Language: The Representational Function of Language*. Transl. by D. F. Goodwin. Amsterdam: John Benjamins.

Burton, D. 1980. *Dialogue and Discourse: A Sociolinguistic Approach to Modern Drama Dialogue and Naturally Occurring Conversation*. London: Routledge and Kegan Paul.

Burton, D. 1981. Analysing spoken discourse. In *Studies in Discourse Analysis*, M. Coulthard & M. Montgomery (eds), 61–81. London: Routledge and Kegan Paul.

Butler, C. S. 1988. Pragmatics and systemic linguistics. *Journal of Pragmatics* 12: 83–102.

Carter, R. 1988. Vocabulary, cloze and discourse. In *Vocabulary and Language Teaching*, R. Carter & M. McCarthy (eds), 161–180. London: Longman.

Carter, R. 1998. *Vocabulary: Applied Linguistic Perspectives*, 2nd edn. London: Routledge.

Carter, R. & McCarthy, M. 1995. Grammar and the spoken language. *Applied Linguistics* 16: 141–158.

Carter, R. & McCarthy, M. 2006. *The Cambridge Grammar of English: A Comprehensive Guide to Spoken and Written Grammar and Usage*. Cambridge: CUP.

Carter, R. & Adolphs, S. 2007 Linking the verbal and visual: New directions for corpus linguistics. In *Language in Context: Papers in Honour of Michael Stubbs,* O. Mason & A. Gerbig (eds), 131–147, Tubingen: University of Tubingen Press.

Channell, J. 1994. *Vague Language*. Oxford: OUP.

Cheng, W. & Warren, M. 1999. Facilitating a description of intercultural conversations: The Hong Kong corpus of conversational English. *ICAME Journal 23: 5–20.*

Cheng, W. & Warren, M. 2000. The Hong Kong corpus of spoken English: Language learning through language description. In *Rethinking Language Pedagogy from a Corpus Perspective: Papers from the Third International Conference on Teaching and Language Corpora*, L. Burnard & T. McEnery (eds), 133–144. Frankfurt: Lang.

Cheng, W. & Warren, M. 2002. // ↘↗beef ball // → you like //: The Intonation of Declarative-Mood Questions in a Corpus of Hong Kong English. *Teanga* 21: 151–165.

Chomsky, N. 1965. *Aspects of the Theory of Syntax*. Cambridge MA: The MIT Press.

Christie, F. 1986. Writing in schools: Generic structures as ways of meaning. In *Functional Approaches to Writing Research Perspectives*, B. Couture (ed.), 221–240. London: Pinter.

Clear, J. 1987. A modest proposal: The grammar of speech acts. In *Discussing Discourse*, M. Coulthard (ed.), 63–79. Birmingham: University of Birmingham, English Language Research.

Conrad, S. 2002. Corpus linguistic approaches for discourse analysis. *Annual Review of Applied Linguistics* 22: 75–95.

Cook, G. 1990. Transcribing infinity: Problems of context presentation. *Journal of Pragmatics* 14: 1–24.

Cook, G. 1994. *Discourse and Literature: The Interplay of Form and Mind*. Oxford: OUP.

Cook, G. 1998. The uses of reality: A reply to Ronald Carter. *English Language Teaching Journal* 52: 57–63.

Cotterill, J. 2004. Collocation, connotation and courtroom semantics: Lawyers control of witness testimony through lexical negotiation. *Applied Linguistics* 25: 513–537.

Coulmas, F. 1979. On the sociolinguistic relevance of routine formulae. *Journal of Pragmatics* 3: 239–266.

Coulmas, F. 1981. *Conversational Routine: Explorations in Standardised Communication Situations and Prepatterned Speech*. The Hague: Mouton.

Cowie, A. P. 1981. The treatment of collocations and idioms in learners dictionaries. *Applied Linguistics* 2: 223–235.

Cowie, A. P. 1988. Stable and creative aspects of vocabulary use. In *Vocabulary and Language Teaching*, R. Carter & M. McCarthy (eds), 126–139. London: Longman.

Cowie, A. P. & Mackin, R. (eds). 1975. *Oxford Dictionary of Current Idiomatic English,* Vol. 1: *Verbs with Prepositions and Particles*. London: OUP.

Crabtree, A., French, A., Greenhalgh, C., Benford, S., Cheverst, K., Fitton, D., Rouncefield, M. & Graham, C. 2005. *Developing Digital Records*. Nottingham: e-Social Science Research Node, University of Nottingham.

Craig, R. T. 1990. Multiple goals in discourse: An epilogue. In *Multiple Goals in Discourse*, K. Tracy & N. Coupland (eds), 163–140. Clevedon: Multilingual Matters.

De Beaugrande, R. 1996. The "pragmatics" of doing language science: The "warrant" for large corpus-linguistics. *Journal of Pragmatics* 25: 503–535.

De Cock, S., Granger, S., Leech, G. & McEnery, T. 1998. An automated approach to the phrasicon of EFL learners. In *Learner English on Computer*, S. Granger (ed.), 67–79. London: Longman.

de Saussure, F. 1916/1966. *Course in General Linguistics*. New York NY: McGraw Hill.

DeCapua, A. & Huber, L. 1995. "If I were you...": Advice in American English. *Multilingua* 14: 117–132.

DeClerck, B. 2004. On the pragmatic functions of lets utterances. In *Language and Computers: Advances in Corpus Linguistics*, K. Aijmer & B. Altenberg (eds), 213–233. Amsterdam: Rodopi.

Dörnyei, Z. & Thurrell, S. 1992. *Conversation and Dialogues in Action*. Hemel Hempstead: Prentice Hall.

Dudley- Evans, T. 1994. Genre analysis: An approach to text analysis for ESP. In *Advances in Written Text Analysis*, M. Coulthard (ed.), 219–228. London: Longman.

Duncan, S. 1972. Some signals and rules for taking speaking turns in conversation. *Journal of Personality and Social Psychology* 23: 283–292.

Eggins, S. & Slade, D. 1997. *Analysing Casual Conversation*. London: Cassell.

Eisenstein, M. & Bodman, J. 1986. "I very appreciate": Expressions of gratitude by native and non-native speakers of American English. *Applied Linguistics* 7: 167–185.

Ekman, P. & Friesen, W. V. 1975. *Unmasking the Face. A Guide to Recognizing Emotions from Facial Clues*. Englewood Cliffs NJ: Prentice-Hall.

Erman, B. 2007. Cognitive processes as evidence of the idiom principle. *International Journal of Corpus Linguistics* 12: 25–53.

Esser, J. 1993. *English Linguistic Stylistics*. Tübingen: Niemeyer.

Faerch, C. & Kasper, G. 1989. Internal and external modification in interlanguage request modification. In *Cross-cultural Pragmatics: Requests and Apologies*, S. Blum-Kulka, J. House & G. Kasper (eds), 221–247. Norwood NJ: Ablex.

Farr, F. & OKeeffe, A. 2002. Would as a hedging device in an Irish context. In *Using Corpora to Explore Linguistic Variation*, R. Reppen, S. Fitzmaurice & D. Biber (eds), 25–48. Amsterdam: John Benjamins.

Farr, F., Murphy, B. & OKeeffe, A. 2004. The Limerick corpus of Irish English: Design, description and application. *Teanga* 21: 5–29.

Fernando, C. 1996. *Idioms and Idiomaticity*. Oxford: OUP.

Firth, J. R. 1957. *Papers in Linguistics 1934–1951*. London: OUP.

Fraser, B. 1975. Hedged performatives. In *Syntax and Semantics*, Vol. 3, P. Cole & J. L. Morgan (eds), 187–210. New York NY: Academic Press.

French, A., Greenhalgh, C., Crabtree, A. , Wright, M., Brundell, P., Hampshire, A., & Rodden, T. 2006. Software Replay Tools for Time-based Social Science Data. Paper delivered at the *2nd annual international e-Social Science conference*, June 2006, University of Manchester.

Garcia, C. 1989. Apologizing in English: Politeness strategies used by native and non-native speakers. *Multilingua* 8: 3–20.

Gardner, R. 1997. The listener and minimal responses in conversational interaction. *Prospect* 12(2): 12–32.

Gardner, R. 1998. Between speaking and listening, the vocalization of understandings. *Applied Linguistics* 19: 204–224.

Gardner, R. 2002. *When Listeners Talk: Response Tokens and Listener Stance*. Amsterdam: John Benjamins.

Goffman, E. 1964. The neglected situation. In *American Anthropologist*, J. J. Gumperz & D. Hymes (eds), Vol. 66, no. 6, part 2, 133–136. Menasha WI: American Anthropological Association.

Goffman, E. 1967. *Interaction Ritual: Essays on Face-to-Face Behaviour*. New York NY: Anchor Books.

Goldin-Meadow, S. 1999. The role of gesture in communication and thinking. *Trends in Cognitive Sciences* 3: 419–429.

Goodwin, C. 1981. *Conversational Organization: Interaction between Speakers and Hearers*. New York NY: Academic Press.

Green, G. M. 1972. *Pragmatics and Natural Language Understanding*. Hillsdale NJ: Lawrence Erlbaum Associates.

Greenhalgh, C., French, A., Tennant, P., Humble, J. & Crabtree, A. 2007. From ReplayTool to Digital Replay System, Online Proceedings of the 3rd International Conference on e-Social Science, Ann Arbor MI, October 2007.

Grice, H. P. 1975. Logic and conversation. In *Syntax and Semantics*, Vol. 3, P. Cole & J. L. Morgan (eds), 41–58. New York NY: Academic Press.

Gumperz, J. J. 1992. Contextualization and understanding. In *Rethinking Context: Language as an Interactive Phenomenon*, A. Duranti & C. Goodwin (eds), 229–252. Cambridge: CUP.

Gumperz, J. J. 1977. Sociocultural knowledge in conversational inference. In *Linguistics and Anthropology*, M. Saville-Troike (ed.), 191–211. Washington DC: Georgetown University Press.

Gumperz, J. J. 1982. *Discourse Strategies*. Cambridge: CUP.

Haiman, J. 1998. The metalinguistics of ordinary language. *Evolution of Communication* 2: 117–135.

Halliday, M. A. K. 1970. Language structure and language function. In *New Horizons in Linguistics*, J. Lyons (ed.), 140–165. Harmondsworth: Penguin.

Halliday, M. A. K. 1973. *Explorations in the Functions of Language*. London: Edward Arnold.

Halliday, M. A. K. 1978. *Language as Social Semiotic*. London: Edward Arnold.

Halliday, M. A. K. 1985. *An Introduction to Functional Grammar*. London: Edward Arnold.

Halliday, M. A. K. & Hasan, R. 1976. *Cohesion in English*. London: Longman.

Hammond, J. & Derewianka, B. 2001. Genre. In *The Cambridge Guide to Teaching English to Speakers of Other Languages*, R. Carter & D. Nunan (eds), 186–193. Cambridge: CUP.

Harrison, J. 2001. The Structure of Discussion: A Discourse Analytical Approach to the Identification of Structure in the Text Type Discussion. PhD dissertation, The University of Nottingham.

Hasan, R. 1978. Text in the systemic-functional model. In *Current Trends in Text Linguistics*, W. U. Dressler (ed.), 228–246. Berlin: Walter de Gruyter.

Hasan, R. 1985. The structure of a text. In *Language, Context and Text: Aspects of Language in a Social-semiotic Perspective*, M. A. K. Halliday & R. Hasan (eds), 52–69. Cambridge: CUP.

Hasan, R. 1999. Speaking with reference to context. In *Text and Context in Functional Linguistics*, M. Ghadessy (ed.), 219–328. Amsterdam: John Benjamins.

Heritage, J. & Sefi, S. 1992. Dilemmas of advice: Aspects of delivery and reception of advice in interactions between health visitors and first time mothers. In *Talk at Work: Interaction in Institutional Settings*, P. Drew & J. Heritage (eds), 359–417. Cambridge: CUP.

Hinkel, E. 1997. Appropriateness of Advice: DCT and Multiple Choice Data. *Applied Linguistics* 18: 1–26.

Hoey, M. 1983. *On the Surface of Discourse*. London: Allen and Unwin.

Hoey, M. 2005. *Lexical Priming*. London: Routledge.

Horn, L. R. 1989. *A Natural History of Negation*. Chicago IL: University of Chicago Press.

House, J. 1989. Politeness in English and German: The functions of "please" and "bitte". In *Cross-cultural Pragmatics: Requests and Apologies*, S. Blum-Kulka, J. House & G. Kasper (eds), 96–119. Norwood NJ: Ablex.

House, J. & Kasper, G. 1981. Politeness markers in English and German. In *Conversational Routine: Explorations in Standardized Communication Situations and Prepatterned Speech*, F. Coulmas (ed.), 157–185. The Hague: Mouton.

House, J. & Kasper, G. 1987. Interlanguage pragmatics: Requesting in a foreign language. In *Perspectives on Language in Performance*, Vol. 2, W. Lörscher & R. Schulze (eds), 1250–1288. Tübingen: Narr.

Hudson, T. 1990. The discourse of advice giving in English: "I wouldnt feed until spring no matter what you do". *Language and Communication* 10(4): 285–297.

Hymes, D. 1972. On communicative competence. In *Sociolinguistics*, J. B. Pride & J. Holmes (eds), 269–293. Harmondsworth: Penguin.

Hymes, D. 1973. *Toward Linguistic Competence*. Austin TX: Department of Anthropology, University of Texas.

Hymes, D. 1986. Models of the interaction of language and social life. In *Directions in Sociolinguistics: The Ethnography of Communication*, J. J. Gumperz & D. Hymes (eds), 35–71. Oxford: Blackwell.

Jakobson, R. 1960. Linguistics and poetics. In *Style in Language*, T. A. Sebeok (ed.), 350–377. Cambridge MA: The MIT Press.

Jefferson, G. 1984. On stepwise transition from talk about trouble to inappropriately next-positioned matters. In *Structures of Social Action*, J. M. Atkinson & J. Heritage (eds), 191–222. Cambridge: CUP.

Jefferson, G. & Lee, J. R. E. 1992. The rejection of advice: Managing the problematic convergence of a "trouble telling" and a "service encounter". In *Talk at Work: Interaction in Institutional Settings*, P. Drew & J. Heritage (eds), 521–548. Cambridge: CUP.

Kasper, G. 1990. Linguistic Politeness. *Journal of Pragmatics* 14(2): 193–218.

Keller, E. 1979. Gambits: Conversational Strategy Signals. *Journal of Pragmatics* 3: 219–238.

Kendon, A. 1967. Some functions of gaze-direction in social interaction. *Acta Psychologica* 26(1): 22–63.

Kendon, A. 1972. Some relationships between body motion and speech. In *Studies in Dyadic Communication*, A. W. Siegman & B. Pope (eds), 177–210. New York NY: Pergamon.

Kendon, A. 1994. Do gestures communicate? A review. *Research on Language and Social Interaction* 27: 175–200.

Kendon, A. 1996. An agenda for gesture studies. *Semiotic Review of Books* 7(3): 8–12.

Kendon, A. 1980. Gesticulation and speech: Two aspects of the process of utterance. In *The Relationship of Verbal and Non-verbal Communication*, M. Key (ed.), 207–227. The Hague: Mouton.

Kennedy, G. 1998. *An Introduction to Corpus Linguistics*. London: Longman.

Kirk, D., Crabtree, A. & Rodden, T. 2005. Ways of the hands. In *Proceedings of the 9th European Conference on Computer Supported Cooperative Work*, H. W. Gellersen, K. Schmidt, M. Beaudouin-Lafon & W. Mackay (eds), 1–21. New York NY: Springer.

Knapp, P. 1997. Virtual Grammar: Writing as Affect/Effect. PhD dissertation, University of Technology, Sydney.

Knight, D., Bayoumi, S., Mills, S., Crabtree, A., Adolphs, S., Pridmore, T. & Carter, R. 2006. Beyond the text: Construction and analysis of multi-modal linguistic corpora. In *Proceedings of the 2nd International Conference for e-Social Science*, 28–30 June 2006, University of Manchester.

Köster, A. 2001. Interpersonal Markers in Workplace Genres: Pursuing Transactional and Relational Goals in Office Talk. PhD dissertation, University of Nottingham.

Kress, G. & van Leeuwen, T. 1996. *Reading Images: The Grammar of Visual Design.* London: Routledge.

Kress, G. & van Leeuwen, T. 2001. *Multimodal Discourse: The Modes and Media of Contemporary Communication.* London: Arnold.

Leech, G. 1983. *Principles of Pragmatics.* London: Longman.

Leech, G. 2000. Grammars of spoken English: New outcomes of corpus-oriented research. *Language Learning* 50: 675–724.

Leech, G. & Short, M. 1981. *Style in Fiction,* London: Longman.

Leech, G. & Svartvik, J. (1994). *A Communicative Grammar of English.* Harlow: Longman.

Levinson, S. C. 1983. *Pragmatics.* Cambridge: CUP.

Levinson, S. C. 1992. Activity types and language. In *Talk at Work: Interaction in Institutional Settings,* P. Drew & J. Heritage (eds), 66–100. Cambridge: CUP.

Longacre, R. E. 1976. *An Anatomy of Speech Notions.* Lisse: Peter de Ridder Press.

Longacre, R. E. 1983. *The Grammar of Discourse.* New York NY: Plenum.

Louw, B. 1993. Irony in the text or insincerity in the writer? The diagnostic potential of semantic prosodies. In *Text and Technology: In Honour of John Sinclair,* M. Baker, G. Francis & E. Tognini-Bonelli (eds), 157–176. Amsterdam: John Benjamins.

Malinowski, B. 1923. The problem of meaning in primitive languages. In *The Meaning of Meaning,* C. K. Ogden & I. A. Richards (eds), 296–336. London: Routledge and Kegan Paul.

Manes, J. & Wolfson, N. 1981. The compliment formula. In *Conversational Routine: Exploration in Standardized Communications Situations and Prepatterned Speech,* F. Coulmas (ed.), 115–132. The Hague: Mouton.

Marmaridou, S. 1988. Contrastive analysis at discourse level and the communicative teaching of languages. *Papers and Studies in Contrastive Linguistics* 22: 123–132.

Martin, J. R. & Rothery, J. 1986. *Writing Project Report* No. 4. [Working Papers in Linguistics]. Sydney: Linguistics Department.

Martin, J. R. 1988. Hypotactic recursive systems in English: Towards a functional interpretation. In *Systemic Functional Approaches to Discourse: Selected Papers from the 12th International Systemic Workshop,* J. D. Benson & W. S. Greaves (eds), 240–270. Norwood NJ: Ablex.

Martin, J. R. 1989. *Factual Writing: Exploring and Challenging Social Reality.* Oxford: OUP.

Maynard, S. K. 1989. *Japanese Conversation: Self-contextualization through Structure and Interactional Management.* Norwood NJ: Ablex.

Maynard, Senko K. 1990. Conversation management in contrast: Listener response in Japanese and American English. *Journal of Pragmatics* 14: 397–412.

Maynard, Senko K. 1997. Analysing interactional management in native/non-native English conversation: A case of listener response. *IRAL* 35: 37–60.

McCarthy, M. 1998. *Spoken Language and Applied Linguistics.* Cambridge: CUP.

McCarthy, M. 2000. Captive audiences: Small talk and close contact service encounters. In *Small Talk,* J. Coupland (ed.), 84–109. Harlow: Longman.

McCarthy, M. 2002. Good listenership made plain: British and American non-minimal response tokens in everyday conversation. In *Using Corpora to Explore Linguistic Variation,* R. Reppen, S. Fitzmaurice & D. Biber (eds), 49–71. Amsterdam: John Benjamins.

McCarthy, M. 2003. Talking back: "Small" interactional response tokens in everyday conversation. *Research on Language and Social Interaction* 36: 33–63.

McClave, E. Z. 2000. Linguistic functions of head movements in the context of speech. *Journal of Pragmatics* 32(7): 855–878.

Mitchell, A. G. 1957. *Spoken English*. London: Macmillan.

Moon, R. 1994. The analysis of fixed expressions in text. In *Advances in Written Text Analysis*, M. Coulthard (ed.), 117–135. London: Routledge.

Moon, R. 1997. Vocabulary connections: Multi-word items in English. In *Vocabulary: Description, Acquisition and Pedagogy*, N. Schmitt & M. McCarthy (eds), 40–63. Cambridge: CUP.

Moon, R. 1998. *Fixed Expressions and Idioms in English: A Corpus-based Approach*. Oxford: Claredon.

Morgan, J. L. 1978. Two types of convention in indirect speech acts. In *Syntax and Semantics* 9: *Pragmatics*, P. Cole (ed.), 261–280. New York NY: Academic Press.

Morrow, P. R. 2006. Telling about problems and giving advice in an Internet discussion forum: Some discourse features. *Discourse Studies* 8(4): 531–548.

Mott, H. & Petrie, H. 1995. Workplace interactions: Womens linguistic behaviour. *Journal of Social Psychology* 14: 324–336.

Munby, J. 1978. *Communicative Syllabus Design*. Cambridge: CUP.

Nattinger, J. R. & DeCarrico, J. S. 1989. Lexical phrases, speech acts and teaching conversation. *AILA Review* 6: 118–139.

Nattinger, J. R. & Decarrico, J. S. 1992. *Lexical Phrases and Language Teaching*. Oxford: OUP.

OKeeffe, A. 2006. *Investigating Media Discourse*. London: Routledge.

OKeeffe, A. 2007. The pragmatics of corpus linguistics. Plenary talk presented at the Corpus Linguistics conference, 27–29 July 2007, University of Birmingham, UK.

OKeeffe, A. & Adolphs, S. Forthcoming. Using a corpus to look at variational pragmatics: Response tokens in British and Irish discourse. In *Variational Pragmatics*, K. P. Schneider & A. Barron (eds). Amsterdam: John Benjamins.

ODonnell, M. 1990. A dynamic model of exchange. *Word* 41: 293–327.

Olshtain, E. 1983. Sociocultural competence and language transfer: The case of apology. In *Language Transfer in Language Learning*, S. Gass & L. Selinker (eds), 232–249. Rowley MA: Newbury House.

Olshtain, E. 1989. Apologies across cultures. In *Cross-cultural Pragmatics: Requests and Apologies*, S. Blum-Kulka, J. House & G. Kasper (eds), 155–173. Norwood NJ: Ablex.

Pawley, A. & Syder, F., H. 1983. Two puzzles for linguistic theory: Native-like selection and native-like fluency. In *Language and Communication*, J. C. Richards & R. W. Schmidt (eds), 191–226. Harlow: Longman.

Platinga, E. O. 1987. The processing of metaphor by computer. In *Metaphor, Communication and Cognition* [Monograph series of the Toronto Semiotic Circle 2], M. Danesi (ed.), 23–47. Toronto: University of Toronto.

Plum, G. A. 1988. Text and Contextual Conditioning in Spoken English: A Genre-based Approach. PhD dissertation, University of Sydney.

Reppen, R., Fitzmaurice, S. & Biber, D. (eds). 2002. *Using Corpora to Explore Linguistic Variation*. Amsterdam: John Benjamins.

Roger, D. B., & Nesshoever, W. 1987. Individual differences in dyadic conversational strategies: A further study. *British Journal of Social Psychology* 26: 247–255.

Sacks, H. 1992. *Lectures on Conversation*. Oxford: Blackwell.

Sacks, H., Schegloff, E. A. & Jefferson, G. 1974. A simplest systematics for the organisation of turn-taking for conversation. *Language* 50: 696–735.

Sadock, J. M. 1974. *Toward a Linguistic Theory of Speech Acts*. New York NY: Academic Press.

Sag, I. A., Baldwin, T., Bond, F., Copestake, A. & Flickinger, D. 2002. Multiword expressions: A pain in the neck for NLP. In *Proceedings of the 3rd International Conferences on Intelligent Text Processing and Computational Linguistics*, A. Gelbukh (ed.), 1–15. London: Springer.

Schauer, G. A. & Adolphs, S. 2006. Expressions of gratitude in Corpus and DCT data: Vocabulary, formulaic sequences, and pedagogy. *System* 34(1): 119–134.

Schegloff, E. A. 1982. Discourse as interactional achievement: Some uses of uh huh and other things that come between sentences. In *Analysing Discourse: Text and Talk*, D. Tannen (ed.), 71–93. Washington DC: Georgetown University Press.

Schegloff, E. A. 1984. On some questions and ambiguities in conversation. In *Structures of Social Action: Studies in Conversation Analysis*, J. M. Atkinson & J. Heritage (eds), 28–52. Cambridge: CUP.

Schegloff, E. A. &d Sacks, H. 1973. Opening up closings. *Semiotica* 8: 289–327.

Schmidt, R. W. & Richards, J. C. 1980. Speech acts and second language learning. *Applied Linguistics* 1: 129–157.

Schmitt, N. (ed.). 2004. *Formulaic Sequences: Acquisition, Processing and Use*. Amsterdam: John Benjamins.

Searle, J. (ed.). 1971. *Philosophy of Language*. Oxford: OUP.

Searle, J. 1969. *Speech Acts: An Essay in the Philosophy of Language*. Cambridge: CUP.

Searle, J. 1975. Indirect speech acts. In *Syntax and Semantics*, Vol. 3, P. Cole & J. L. Morgan (eds), 59–82. New York NY: Academic Press.

Searle, J. 1976. The classification of illocutionary acts. *Language in Society* 5: 1–24.

Semino, E. & Short, M. 2004. *Corpus stylistics: Speech, Writing and Thought Presentation in a Corpus of English Narratives*. London: Routledge.

Simpson, P. 1993. *Language, Ideology and Point of View*, London: Routledge.

Simpson, R., Lucka, B. & Ovens, J. 2000. Methodological challenges of planning a spoken corpus with pedagogical outcomes. In *Rethinking Language Pedagogy from a Corpus Perspective: Papers from the Third International Conference on Teaching and Language Corpora*, L. Burnard & T. McEnery (eds), 43–49. Frankfurt: Lang.

Sinclair, J. M. 1987. Collocation: A progress report. In *Language Topics: Essays in Honour of Michael Halliday*, R. Steele & T. Threadgold (eds), 319–331. Amsterdam: John Benjamins.

Sinclair, J. M. 1991. *Corpus, Concordance, Collocation*. Oxford: OUP.

Sinclair, J. M. 1992. Priorities in discourse analysis. In *Advances in Spoken Discourse Analysis*, M. Coulthard (ed.), 79–88. London: Routledge.

Sinclair, J. M. 1996. The search for the units of meaning. *Textus* 9(1): 75–106.

Sinclair, J. M. 2004. *Trust the Text: Language Corpus and Discourse*. London: Routledge.

Sinclair, J. M. 2004 [1996]. The search for the units of meaning. In *Trust the Text: Language Corpus and Discourse*, 24–48. London: Routledge.

Sinclair, J. M. & Coulthard, M. 1975. *Towards an Analysis of Discourse*. London: OUP.

Spencer-Oatey, H. & Zegarac, V. 2002. Pragmatics. In *An Introduction to Applied Linguistics*, N. Schmitt (ed.), 74–91. London: Arnold.

Sperber, D. & Wilson, D. 1986. *Relevance: Communication and Cognition*. Oxford: Blackwell.

Stenström, A. B. 1990. Lexical items peculiar to spoken discourse. In *The London-Lund Corpus of Spoken English: Description and Research*, J. Svartvik (ed.), 137–175. Lund: Lund University Press.

Stockley, S. 2006. The Development of an Analytical Tool for Automated Dialogue Act Annotation of Spoken Corpora. PhD dissertation, Lancaster University.

Strässler, J. 1982. *Idioms in English: A Pragmatic Analysis*. Tübingen: Narr.

Stubbs, M. 1983a. *Discourse Analysis: The Sociolinguistic Analysis of Natural Language*. Oxford: Blackwell.

Stubbs, M. 1983b. Can I have that in writing, please? Some neglected topics in speech act theory. *Journal of Pragmatics* 7: 479–494.

Stubbs, M. 1995. Collocations and semantic profiles: On the cause of the trouble with quantitative methods. *Functions of Language* 2(1): 1–33.

Stubbs, M. 1996. *Text and Corpus Analysis: Computer-Assisted Studies of Language and Culture*. Oxford: Blackwell.

Stubbs, M. 2001. *Words and Phrases: Corpus Studies of Lexical Semantics*. Oxford: Blackwell.

Svartvik, J. 1980. Well in conversation. In *Studies in English Linguistics for Randolph Quirk*, S. Greenbaum, G. Leech & J. Svartvik (eds), 167–177. London: Longman.

Swales, J. M. 1990. *Genre Analysis: English in Academic and Research Settings*. Cambridge: CUP.

Swales, J. M. 2004. *Research Genres: Explorations and Applications*. Cambridge: CUP.

Tannen, D. (ed.). 1993. *Framing in Discourse*. Oxford: OUP.

Thibault, P. J. & van Leeuwen, T. 1996. Grammar, society and the speech act: Renewing the connections. *Journal of Pragmatics* 25: 561–585.

Thompson, P. 2005. Spoken language corpora. In *Developing Linguistic Corpora: A Guide to Good Practice*, M. Wynne (ed), 59–70. Oxford: Oxbow Books.

Tognini-Bonelli, E. & Manca, E. 2004. Welcoming children, pets and guests: Towards functional equivalence in the languages of "Agriturismo" and "Farmhouse Holidays". In *Language and Computers: Advances in Corpus Linguistics*, K. Aijmer & B. Altenberg (eds), 371–385. Amsterdam: Rodopi.

Tracy, K. & Coupland, N. (eds). 1990. *Multiple Goals in Discourse*. Clevedon: Multilingual Matters.

Tsui, A. 1994. *English Conversation*. Oxford: OUP.

van Dijk, T. A. 1982. Episodes as units of discourse analysis. In *Analyzing Discourse: Text and Talk*, D. Tannen (ed.), 177–195. Washington DC: Georgetown University Press.

van Lancker, D., Canter, G. J. & Terbeek, D. 1981. Disambiguation of ditropic sentences: Acoustic and phonetic cues. *Journal of Speech and Hearing Research* 24: 330–335.

Ventola, E. 1987. *The Structure of Social Interaction: A Systemic Approach to the Semiotics of Service Encounters*. London: Pinter.

Verschueren, J. 1981. The semantics of forgotten routines. In *Conversational Routines*, F. Coulmas (ed.), 133–153. The Hague: Mouton.

Weinreich, U. 1980. Problems in the analysis of idioms. In *On Semantics*, W. Labov & B. Weinreich (eds), 208–264. Philadelphia PA: University of Pennsylvania Press.

Weisser, M. 2003. SPAACy- A semi-automated tool for annotating dialogue acts. *International Journal of Corpus Linguistics 8: 63–74*.

Wood, D. 2006. Uses and functions of formulaic sequences in second language speech: An exploration of the foundations of fluency. *The Canadian Modern Language Review* 63: 13–33.

Woods, A., Fletcher, P. & Hughes, A. 1986. *Statistics in Language Studies*. Cambridge: CUP.

Wray, A. 2002. *Formulaic Language and the Lexicon*. Cambridge: CUP.

Yngve, V. H. 1970. On getting a word in edgewise. In *Proceedings of the 6th Regional Meeting of the Chicago Linguistic Society*, 567–577. Chicago IL: Chicago Linguistic Society.

Index

In the series *Studies in Corpus Linguistics (SCL)* the following titles have been published thus far or are scheduled for publication: